CW00860462

For Jen, who was always at the end of the phone when I got lost, who taught me that everything would be ok, and who understood me even when I didn't

For Charles, who taught me that marriage is not about 50/50 but about giving what you can and who showed me what real love is.

And, for Zoe and Lily, who are my heart, my sunshine, my inspiration, my everything.

PROLOGUE

I was exhausted, freezing and my eyes were raw from crying but I was ready for a fight. After packing a bag, spending 6 hours in a hospital gown on a gurney in the hall of the emergency room and begging, then bullying, the ER psychiatrist to admit me to the psych ward, I was full of venom.

I had not been eating for months. I had no energy, I was feeling faint in the office, I couldn't concentrate. I would crawl to the train every night, promising myself that once I sat down, my heart flutters would stop. I started to feel depressed; I lied about how I was doing. I withdrew from the world – from my family, from my husband (Charles), from my daughters (Zoe and Lily) and from my friends – canceling plans at the last minute, keeping to myself, becoming uncommunicative. Some days, I had to work from home because I could not face leaving the house.

All of that would have been worth it, or so I thought, if only it would help me lose more weight. But, no matter how much I cut out eating wise, the scale just wouldn't budge. I felt hopeless, like nothing mattered anymore. I felt like I could not carry on. I thought I wanted to die. But really, I just wanted the pain to stop.

I didn't know how to pretend anymore.

I didn't want to hear that I belonged at the Douglas Eating Disorder Program. I had flunked out of their "food school" (officially known as Day Hospital Treatment) months before; I most definitely did not want to hear that recovery takes time and that it is not linear. After all, I had been living with anorexia on and off for 17 years. I knew better than most that it was not linear and that it was much closer to a marathon than a sprint. I didn't want to hear any of it.

All I wanted was to be saved.

I threatened to act on my suicidal thoughts or even to start taking drugs so that I could go to rehab – all so that someone would admit me somewhere. I was desperate for someone to take me by the hand and lock me away until I was fixed.

Now, to be fair, I was not being denied treatment. In fact, the doctor was strongly recommending I seek treatment at the Eating Disorder Program. But I was not being given the treatment that I thought I needed: hospitalization. I felt let down, and angry. I had finally allowed myself to be vulnerable and ask for help and I felt I was being turned away for not being sick enough.

Then, broken, lost and defeated, I stopped fighting and accepted the help being offered to me. I was numb, I was skeptical and I had no idea what would happen next. The only thing I knew was that I needed and wanted to recover. I was afraid of getting better. But even more than that, I was petrified that if I did not get help right now, I would change my mind and go back to my pattern of convincing myself and others that things weren't that bad.

I spent the next few days in a daze. Head down, I humbly had to ask the Eating Disorder Clinic I had openly criticized to accept me back into their treatment program; I had to explain things to my parents, to my husband and to my friends. But, most of all, I had to try something different. I couldn't keep doing what I had been doing – hit a low point, get motivated to change only to lose steam after a few weeks or months, and then start the cycle all over again.

I signed up to go live in a Crisis Center for a few days so that I could have access to support 24/7. I knew I was fragile and that if I was not careful, I would either lose my nerve to start eating again or, worse, I would let the darkness take over for good.

So, I packed a bag, not knowing when exactly I would be home. I lied to my daughters (who are 7 and 5) and said I was going on a business trip and I told my colleagues I was ill (greater truth was never told). I drove myself to the Crisis Center on autopilot. I had no idea what to expect and I honestly didn't have the energy to spend time worrying about what would come. I handed over my medication so they could keep it under lock and key and I settled into my room.

Expectations were made clear at the onset:

1. I was expected to set daily objectives and sit down with the social worker to discuss them;

2. I was expected to help cook and eat dinner with everyone in the house every night; and

3. I was not allowed to starve the rest of the day.

Naps were limited, TV was prohibited until 4 pm and hot water was scarce.

I took this all in and felt elated. Somehow I knew deep down that this was just what I needed. A place to re-boot my brain, where help was being imposed on me so that I didn't have to find the courage to ask for it. I was in a place where accepting the support offered was a requirement and not a choice. This gave me the freedom to focus my energy away from fighting the guilt of needing help to simply fighting my eating disorder.

It was a wakeup call of sorts – with none of my creature comforts or my restriction enablers – and not a single second of escape from the reality that I was in a bad place. You can pretend when you are home…escaping to the magical world of Netflix. It is not so easy to do when you are listening to the life stories of the people I met at the Crisis Center.

I looked at the clock. 10:00…Kids were at school; most people were at work. Normally, I would wait a further 2 hours before I would allow myself to consume anything other than water, coffee or gum. But, I went down to the communal kitchen and found some cinnamon raisin bread.

I put a slice in the toaster and, once ready, closed my eyes, took a deep breath and had my first bite.

It was only a slice of toast - whose calorie content was well-known to me; it would hardly make a dent on my weight but it was the beginning of my recovery...where I would systematically break down every restriction rule I had written for myself...starting with bread for breakfast.

This was the day I started eating...

Gladiatorin4inchheels.com

THE SHOW

When I was a little girl, I wanted to be many things: nurse, teacher, actress. As the years went on, I realized I was too squeamish to be a nurse, too impatient to be a teacher, and way too shy to be an actress.

And, while I still lack the personality or skill to be an actress, it turns out I am quite skilled at putting on a show.

Putting on a brave face, being open about my challenges while making light of them at the same time, pretending to be Wonder Woman....everything cleverly crafted to give the impression that, while things are tough at times these days, I'm ok.

Turns out, I've been putting on such a great show that I even convinced myself...until I no longer had the strength to keep up the performance – even for myself.

So, after a bit of an intervention of sorts with a Wise friend (that's you, Heather), a guiding hand from James up above (via you, Josee) and a caring Husband, the curtain came down this weekend.

So...I am going to take a break from performing for a little bit. I am going to put this blog on hiatus – just for a little while. But I'll be back. And I am sure there will be lots to tell.

Peiky out...for now...

(Note: written right before the day I started eating)

IS THIS BOOK FOR YOU?

I am impatient. I don't sit still for very long, preferring to fill my time with actions. And when I move, I like to move quickly. Needless to say, I hate wasting time and effort. So, when I started treatment for my Eating Disorder, I had specific expectations.

I was ready to put my all into recovery but I expected things to progress quickly. I did not want to spend time on treatment activities that I didn't believe would work. I wanted to know exactly what I was doing and how it would help. The clock was ticking and I wasn't prepared to misuse my time.

Of course, it doesn't work that way...

Still, for those of you who are similar to me, let's get right to it and answer the key question that my former self would be asking right now: "is this the right book for me? Is it worth my time and energy?"

Well, that all depends on the type of person you are, where you are in your recovery and what you are looking for in your life right now.

I spent a year trying to learn everything I could about anorexia, low self-esteem, changing habits and finding happiness. I read every book I could put my hands on. After each one, I felt energized. I knew what I needed to do...then, within a few days or weeks, the effects would fade and I would read a new one, leaving most of my previous learnings behind. And the cycle continued.

I became frustrated by these starts and stops. How many more books would I have to read? Why couldn't there be a one-stop shop? Where was the book that contained all the key insights I needed? Where was my literary magic pill?

The answer, quite simply, is that there wasn't one. At least not for me. So after spending hours soaking up prose on eating disorders, anxiety, shame, control and self-love, I decided it might be time to consolidate my own learning and see how everything fit together.

This book combines the bits and pieces of everything I read and learned through therapy and fellow Eating Disorder (ED) patients that, only once combined, really helped me move forward.

Great! You think. I'm so happy for you. But what about me? How will this book help me?

I cannot say it will... at least not for sure. But, if you have any of the following characteristics, odds are this book will help you feel understood and, hopefully, armed for the battle ahead:

* Performance-driven
* An insecure over-achiever
* Action-oriented
* Thrives on making plans and following steps
* Motivated by setting and meeting objectives

This book covers the various factors and elements that fueled my anorexia and stopped me from moving forward. It is organized by theme and not by chronology so do not be surprised if the timeline jumps around throughout. I will share how I gained insight into these various areas, and I will try to demystify them. Going beyond the conceptual, it will also provide actions, hints and tips that I followed in order to change the way I behaved and, ultimately, change the way I saw the world.

Throughout each chapter, I will explore the various obstacles to my recovery, how I learned from them and overcame them. I will also share a Blog post that I feel provides a snapshot into the issue. I started writing a Blog about a year ago to share candid moments throughout my recovery. These posts are honest glimpses of my journey which I hope will help you better understand my personal battle toward recovery.

Let's take a moment for an aside on the Blog. For people who know me well, the name - gladiatorin4inchheels - is self-explanatory. But, it might not be so obvious to all readers. I chose this name because I battle my Eating Disorder daily; and high heels are an important part of my armor. I developed a deep love of shoes over a decade ago. Why? Well, superficially, because they are pretty and help me feel beautiful as a result. But, more importantly, they fuel my confidence and sense of inner power - something every Gladiator needs, no?

Now back to the structure of the book. Because I feel the best way to learn is by doing, I have provided an activity to try at the end of each section. Hopefully, each of these will help you tackle the issue described in the Chapter. Some of these are activities I did myself; others are things that, looking back, I think would have been useful to do. Try them, add your own little twist or simply skip them. It really is up to you. But, if you think they sound crazy, maybe that is reason enough to give them a try.

The book should be easy to pick up where you left off at any given moment and light enough that you can binge read without getting a headache.

If you are a doer, a fixer, someone who defines themselves by accomplishing things, this book should speak to you.

Naysayers might think this is a superficial approach to recovery. And, in a way, it is...in the beginning. But it is not forever. For me, I needed a plan to follow; I needed daily objectives and targets to keep me moving while I learned to listen to my body, while I adapted to feeding my body again and started to learn intuitive eating. These activities and objectives were a very useful crutch that I used in order to keep moving while I healed my mind, my body and some old wounds that were buried deep.

In time, I no longer needed the lessons contained in this book…at least not as daily reminders or daily challenges to be completed.

And, while this book has been written from the point of view of someone who has lived with anorexia for almost 2 decades, I think it can be appreciated by a wider audience.

If you know and care about a goal-oriented, insecure overachiever with an Eating Disorder, someone who seems unstoppable regardless of how thin they are or how little they eat (what I call a high-functioning Anorexic), this book can help you understand what they are living and support them in implementing the learnings contained within these pages.

So…enough talk about what this book is or isn't. Let's get started. There is work to be done.

Activity 1: Bullseye

Set yourself at least one objective of what you would like to get out of reading this book. Write it down in the inside cover. It can be as simple as relieving some of your boredom to something more life-changing. It doesn't matter. Just keep this objective close and refer back to it every once in a while to see if it is hitting the mark. If so, I'm glad and I encourage you to keep reading. If not, well, thanks for visiting.

Gladiatorin4inchheels.com

BEAUTIFUL

Yup, after a lot of interesting moments over the last 2 years, I finally look in the mirror and see beauty.

For the first time in a long time, maybe ever, I see myself as beautiful. Sure I see the imperfections, but I see beauty nonetheless.

But wait! Don't organize a parade because there is a slight problem.

Whereas I see beauty, my medical team sees underweight. Hmmm, there's an unexpected dilemma.

What do you do when you have worked so hard to accept yourself and embrace who you are but it remains unhealthy? When you are finally comfortable in your own skin but your thoughts remain focused on restriction and remaining thin?

How do you push yourself to eat more when you firmly believe you are just right. Healthy or happy…that is the question…because both seem impossible.

If you are reading this, hoping for a magical and insightful answer, I am sorry to disappoint because I have nothing.

Every day that I look in the mirror and feel confident and beautiful feels like a gift. So, I have no idea what motivation could propel me to rock this fragile boat.

Some say you have to keep gaining and learn to see beauty at each phase. To that I say a very dubious… « okay»…

I don't believe it and I don't want to. Honestly, I have no desire to trade this contentment for the uncertainty of weight gain and self help.

The therapists say, you don't know until you try and that worst case, I can always lose the weight if I am unhappy.

Gladiatorin4inchheels.com

To that, I say: « bullshit! » The prospect of starvation is no longer an option for me.

Maybe it works for some but I refuse to use that as my plan B.

So instead, i wake up each day, look in the mirror and smile. And if it means I eat just enough to stay at this weight, i will take it…for now.

Cause god knows I have worked hard to get to this place and feeling beautiful is something I am not quite ready to gamble away.

THE STORY OF ME

When I admit I am living with anorexia, I am often faced with 2 reactions.

First, there is a desire to understand the why behind it. People look for the cause behind persistent willful starvation. It defies logic, doesn't it? If you are hungry, you eat. Simple, right? After all, eating is a basic physiological need; something one does without really thinking – like breathing and sleeping.

Ummm…not quite.

Or, I get a knowing look from the person I am talking to. And, for a minute, I think they understand; that they too have battled against the illness or know someone who has. Usually though, the smile isn't a knowing one at all. Rather, it reveals an assumption that the pressure to be thin in our society has driven me to control everything I eat.

Ah…don't get on the soapbox against dolls, supermodels and fashion magazines just yet please.

The truth is that there are many reasons someone develops anorexia – generally involving a mix of genetic, social, emotional and environmental factors. And the exact blend varies per person.

Anorexia is a complex mental illness with a myriad of causes and triggers. Each time I had a relapse, the context was different, my motivations and behaviours were different and my reaction to my weight gain and recovery was certainly different. Just when I thought I understood my illness, it evolved into something else, eluding my grasp.

When I started to write this book, I debated about sharing too many details about how and why I developed anorexia. I used to think I was so special, so unique that no one could understand my particular experience. I would discredit anyone who had recovered if they did not mirror me perfectly. It was my defense mechanism. I would shy away from the learnings these people could bring to me, telling myself I wasn't like them. I was different so the things that worked for them, wouldn't work for me. Why bother trying?

To be clear, I was completely wrong about this point. There are lessons to learn from every story and from every Gladiator who has fought anorexia. I just didn't want to see it at the time. But I do now.

So, if you are reading this, please give these pages a chance even if you do not recognize yourself in my story. There are elements here that I am sure can help you. So keep an open mind even if there is a part of you that wants to use any argument you have to stay in your bubble - believing that your experience of anorexia is so unique that you are beyond help. Yes, you are special and there is no one like you. And it is true that one-size-fits-all therapy does not exist. But, this does not mean that you cannot gain a few insights from these words, make them your own and move forward.

Ok, enough preamble, let's go back to the beginning. You guessed it, my childhood.

I was a timid and emotional child who thrived on achievement. When I did well, which, luckily enough was fairly often, I soared. I felt an innate sense of pride and I was fueled by the accolades I received from those around me. But when I failed, the disappointment was strong and was almost always accompanied by a torrent of tears. No one seemed to know what to do with a third grader who was inconsolable due to a low mark on an exam. They assumed I must be sick.

I got to know a lot of camp and school nurses in my youth as a result. It wasn't that bad, I suppose. I got Kool-Aid and naps out of it. Still...

In time, performing, doing well, being liked all became strongly linked with my self-esteem. And, since I liked feeling good about myself, I became focused on achieving. Too focused! It became a natural high for me and I rarely stopped to enjoy the moment, simply moving on to the next achievement. Why? In my head, I had to perform well in order to earn love, admiration, and the right to relax. This feeling of having to earn things would eventually play into my Eating Disorder but more on that later.

No one ever told me I needed to be a certain way to earn things and no one made me feel that way. Somehow, the wiring in my brain lead me to draw these conclusions.

Because I needed to achieve to feel good, I would do everything I could to ensure I kept hitting the mark. And I worried...I worried about failing a lot. I was the type of child that could be at the movies and, rather than be focused on the action in front of me, I'd be thinking about the exam question I was sure I got wrong that day. Obsessive thoughts – about homework, about being liked at school, about anything – would wake me up repeatedly in the middle of the night.

I have lived with insomnia throughout most of my life – from when I was in grade school – and never realized that one could close their eyes at night and simply wake up the next morning. I thought waking up several times was typical and I had no idea that my sleep patterns were odd.

To avoid the heartbreak I felt over my perceived failures and to avoid sleepless nights as much as possible, I spent a lot of time and effort studying, practicing, perfecting, planning. And then worrying. This became my daily mode of operation. Achieving to a higher standard was the only way I felt good about myself and performing and doing became my coping mechanism for my anxiety, my fears and my insecurities.

Everything would be ok, if I just kept busy and kept getting the A+. This was my philosophy from grade school all the way to when I earned my University degree.

And, on the whole, this approach served me well. It got me the grades, helped me secure a coveted job straight out of university and propelled me in my career. No one knew the depths of my anxiety, my insecurities or the constant loop of thoughts in my head. I was so good at keeping things hidden, I fooled myself and everyone else around me.

Don't think, don't feel, just do. I felt in control; I tamed my anxiety; I kept the monsters at bay. It seemed to work so well...until it didn't anymore.

In the year after graduation, I got a new job, I moved out on my own, I had my heart broken twice and the working world didn't feed my constant need for positive feedback. I was facing a lot of changes in a short period of time, I felt inadequate in love and I was unsure about my work performance. I was doing so much but had no idea if I was getting "As" in the report card of life. So much was happening all at once and my time-tested coping mechanism of achieving was no longer working. I needed something that made me feel in control again – something that I could excel at – and I found it.

Calorie-counting.

It was perfect. I could start each day with a goal to ground me and end each night with the sweet satisfaction of achieving it...then surpassing it. It happened so gradually that I never felt overcome by hunger and, before I knew it, I was skeletal and completely consumed by anorexia. I moved to London for work but also to run away…to hide from everyone that loved me.

I threw myself into work and starvation and ultimately spent three years in a daze which was fueled by loneliness, anorexia and eventually bulimia. I fainted in a grocery store, made a series of bad decisions, had a relationship with a married man and, by the time I moved back to Montreal, felt completely unlovable. I told no one of the depths I had gone to in the previous years and pretended that everything was fine. I looked fine – albeit heavier than I had ever been – so no one really knew how broken I was inside.

I started dating Charles – the man I would eventually marry – and did my best to "act normal" with respect to eating. I had not told anyone about my bulimia because I was ashamed of the fact that I periodically lost control of my eating. Looking back now, I am certain I could have been honest with him from the first date and he would have been supportive. At the time, though, my disordered eating was a part of me that I despised and was desperate to keep hidden. I guess I had a few lessons to learn; lessons I have captured here in these pages.

Once we moved in together, I had no choice but to change my behavior or risk being "found out". I couldn't starve and I certainly couldn't binge without him noticing. So, in time, my behaviors were normalized and the voices in my head quieted down to whispers – never gone but much easier to ignore.

I started to speak openly about my first battle with an eating disorder…as though talking about it ensured it was firmly in the past. Sadly, this was just the beginning of the roller coaster ride anorexia took me on for over a decade.

For a while, my achievements allowed me once again to keep my Eating Disorder behaviours dormant. But, in times of extreme stress or insecurity, the only thing that seemed to keep me sane was restricting and controlling my food intake. After the birth of my first child, when light postpartum depression hit; after the birth of my second child, when I struggled to cope with the demands of a career and 2 children under the age of 4; when I was extremely unhappy at work after taking on a new job that left me feeling rejected by my old team, undervalued by my new one and terribly alone…each and every time, rather than turn to the people who loved me most, I turned to the warm blanket of anorexia to comfort me, to ground me and to take the edge off of life.

Again, I lost myself and my self-respect, gave my power to others and made some of the worst mistakes of my life. I was diagnosed with depression and anxiety, I started antidepressants, I became suicidal, I went on sick leave, I went in and out of therapy programs and I made three trips to the emergency room because I wanted to disappear. I left a company where I had spent almost two decades building a strong reputation and racking up success after success; and, while things started to get better after that, I simply could not get away from the hold anorexia had on me.

You know the rest…I hit rock bottom, went to a Crisis Center, re-booted and started eating. How did I do it? Keep reading.

Activity 2: The Book of YOU

Think about your own story. How did your ED start? Can you remember when you realized you had an ED? Can you remember when you acknowledged having one? Where are you currently in terms of living with your illness? What big milestones have been a part of your own journey? You do not need to do anything with these reflections. Sometimes, though, it helps to have your own story top of mind as you read through a book like this. Perhaps it will help you draw certain parallels and help you identify a few things that are relevant to your own recovery.

FEAR

Imagine you are petrified of spiders. Your pulse quickens at the very thought of them. You periodically scan your surroundings for them. And if you see one, you scream and run away.

Now imagine getting up 4 days a week and driving to a house infested with spiders to conquer your fears with 14 other people who are also petrified of the same thing. You talk about your fears, looking for the underlying causes, share coping mechanisms, and make conversation just to get through the day. Then, at predetermined times in the day, you have to hold a variety of spiders. Some may be "cuter" than others, easier to tolerate. Then you go home and it feels as though spiders are crawling on your skin. You feel them, you smell them, you cannot escape them.

Being in the Day Program and, now the Day Hospital, is very similar. With a few important differences. Instead of arachnids, you are deathly afraid of food and of gaining weight. And, unlike spiders that you can generally ignore, you need food to survive. You cannot call your husband to kill your snack for you. And, your fear is one that people cannot understand. "But food is so good! How can you not like it? Just eat! Spiders are gross, I get it. But food…what is wrong with you?"

The Day Hospital is simply an extension of the Day Program. Rather than leave at 3:30, you stay an additional 4 hours, where you get to cook and eat an additional meal and dessert. 2 snacks, 2 meals and 2 desserts each day. Every bite is a challenge in itself. And there is no escaping. No running 6 km to feel lighter, no sit-ups, no skipping meals – causing feelings of panic about weight gain. You leave full to the brim, exhausted and you smell like food – an inescapable reminder of what you ate. I have only been in Day Hospital for a few days but I go home every night and scrub thoroughly to exorcise the smell.

And then suddenly, you have three days off. Three days where no one else is there to put the metaphorical spider in your hand six times a day; where you could spend all your time running and hiding and focused on other more pleasant things; where you can revert back to your old ways and feel safe and warm. You know you shouldn't. One, because it will just lengthen the battle but also because even one minute of running can erode the tolerance you built up during the week, leaving you skidding down the mountain.

And even though you know restriction is illogical; if you know you won't gain ten pounds in a week; if you know you could get "kicked out" of the program; if you know you will disappoint the people you love; if deep down you want to get well; the fears and urges are strong – like a current whispering your name, waiting to pull you under. So you spend your three days trying to use logic to battle irrational fear.

Fear is powerful. My fear of gaining weight often manifests itself in logical arguments. "No no no, the pancakes are too big even for the average person. It is wasteful. You don't wanna do that. Have the biscuit and fruit with jam….see you are fine; you are eating jam."

Then BAM! The scale gives you the score for your weekly battle. And though it does not always rule in your favour, you know how hard you've battled. And no amount in kilos can take that away from you. You have to find whatever you can to fuel the next weekly fight.

THE ILLUSION OF CONTROL

I can be a control freak. Ok, maybe I am exaggerating. I certainly don't fit the clinical definition. And there are some elements in my life that I have little interest in and am very happy to delegate to others (managing my finances, for example). Perhaps a better way of saying it is that I like to control certain areas of my life. Feeling in control of these areas calms me down. No doubt, this is why I was drawn to anorexia. And, for a long time, I thought it was what explained why I sabotaged my recovery. I was sure that my intense restriction proved I was the master of control, and so I felt safe only when I controlled everything I ate.

"Why?" you might ask. Quite simply restriction gave me a high. Being functional while eating very little made me feel invincible. And, I struggled to admit it, but it made me feel extremely proud. I kept two running tallies during my day: everything I accomplished (laundry, blogging, shopping, dancing with the girls, etc.) and every calorie I consumed. At the end of the day I compared both and the more I was able to get done with the lowest food intake, the greater the level of pride. It was not enough to accomplish a lot in a given day; I had to do this by overcoming severe hunger, fatigue and feeling faint. I needed battle scars in order to earn my daily badge of honor. Much like in my childhood, I needed to feel I had achieved and earned in order to truly feel good about myself.

Feeling in control has always been reassuring the me. If I control everything, nothing can surprise me, nothing can hurt me. Being in control makes me feel like everything will be ok. If I keep all things in check, I'll be fine. I cannot imagine a world without being in the driver's seat of life. Of course, it is a delusion because no one is in full control of everything. In fact, it turns out that I control far less than I allowed myself to believe.

My deep-rooted need to orchestrate my life fully means that I am deathly afraid of losing control.

When it came to eating, I was petrified of giving in to my hunger, buckling under the fatigue and going crazy. This fueled my restrictive tendencies, especially during recovery. When I started eating, it felt like a beast was awakened in me and I felt a raging hunger. I thought the only way to ensure I didn't go overboard was by simply not eating at all. I continually walked a fine line between utter control and having the flood gates open and being crushed by the waves.

The more I felt out of control, the more I desperately tried to dictate and restrict. Until I started to truly recover, I lived unaware of this fact and clung to the belief that I was fully in control.

But then I went to the world's worst dinner party and the illusion came crashing down. I finally realized that I was in denial and spiraling out of control. Trust me. You are not in control when you are anorexic. You only think you are.

If you find solace in being in control, it will be very difficult for you to let go. I hate to say it but long-term recovery and control simply don't mix very well. For me, allowing a bit of unpredictability in my life opened me up to new possibilities and helped change my way of thinking and behaving. Not always…and certainly not instinctually. But, enough to allow me to be able to change my mind even when my initial reaction is one of inflexibility.

Activity 3: Let it Go

The interesting thing about control is that every time you relinquish a bit, it gets easier and easier to do it again.

Do one thing every day that is out of your control. Write a list of activities you can do on a given day. I suggest you include safer activities as well as bolder ones. Cut up a bunch of pieces of paper and put an activity from your list on each one. Fold them up and put them in a jar, a hat, a bowl, anything you can draw from.

Wake up each day, pick a paper and do the activity. No cheating allowed. Write about it in your journal. How did you feel before, during and after? Try to measure your feelings over time.

Need inspiration? Here are a few ideas:

*Go to the movies and see whatever is showing

*Spend a few hours at Starbucks, reading, people watching

*Take a cooking class

*Eat a forbidden food

*Go to the park and swing with abandon

*Dance in public

*Do a paint night

Gladiatorin4inchheels.com

ILL vs WILL

Recently, we were invited for dinner at Charles' colleague's house. Plan was to go over with our girls, have our collective brood play together and enjoy a lovely homecooked meal. What could be nicer, right? Nice people, children taking care of themselves, adult conversation, nothing to cook and no dishes to clean.

As the evening approached though, I started to get nervous. What if they make something I don't like. Let's face it, with my long list of inedible items, there was a high probability this would happen. What about the pressure to be polite and eat my full plate?

Sensitive to my plight, Charles had already inquired on the evening's planned menu: pasta with Cajun chicken. I instantly felt myself relax a bit. Ok, I thought, the type of food is out of the way, you can always warn them when you get there that you are not feeling well and a tiny portion will do for you.

All was going well until drinks were served. Our hostess, proud to have us over, made her famous bourbon lemonade in Mason Jar glasses. Lemonade???? With alcohol??? My mental calculator instantly came to life. 130 calories for can of fizzy lemon… I don't drink bourbon so have no idea about calories…and look at the size of this glass…agh….
So as I nursed my drink, we made conversation. I felt ok. A bit out of my comfort zone but ok. Until I heard the wife ask her husband for 2 containers of cream.

Ummmm. Cream….Now the warning bells were ringing and anxiety and dread were building. I told myself to breathe…we could solve this…Surely we could say I was allergic to dairy…lactose intolerant? But, what if Charles already said I had no allergies. And I can't really ask him in front of them.

Maybe it is for a cream soup…and I can skip the appetizer. Or, if it is a sauce, I can just ask for no sauce. All this is going on in my head as I have a smile plastered on my face. As dinner is being served, the children are watching a movie. How I wish I could just say, "you know what, I'm good, I'll just watch the movie, skip the dinner. You guys enjoy though."

But I know my manners and cannot embarrass myself like that, or Charles.

So I sit down…Not too much wine for me please…(calories). Oh beet salad…I can do this. Wait, there is cheese grated on it, anxiety rises, breathe…ok, ok, just scrape it off. Phew. Time for the main event. I think I'll be ok. Chicken, no sauce, pasta. I see her sprinkle some cheese on the pasta but I think I can handle that.

And then the plate is coming toward me, and lands at my place setting. For everyone else, it looks beautiful. But I want to cry. The chicken has been cooked in the cream sauce. So while the sauce is on the side, as Charles discretely requested for me, I have no choice but to eat it. At this point, I panic internally. I feel trapped. I cannot eat this…options from running out of the house (I could sit sipping a diet coke at the Harveys across the street), to pretending to faint cross my mind. But I can't do that.

So I have a few bites of chicken, trying to wipe the sauce off on my plate. I have some salad even though there is feta in it and I know that no matter how much I try to eat around it, some tiny bits will wind up in my mouth. And I ask for more wine, just to be able to dull the storm going on within me.

At this point, while physically there, I am gone. I zone out. I look around the table at everyone eating, talking, laughing, enjoying the host couple's favorite meal and I want to scream: "what is wrong with you!!!??? How can you sit there, laughing while my skin is crawling. How can you not care about my inner turmoil?"

But how can they know? How can they understand that I am not just picky or weird about food. Unless you are anorexic you cannot understand because anxiety, fear and desperation are not typical reactions to food. But they are for me. And then it hits me. I am not in control at all. It was all an illusion. I now know the Eating Disorder took over long ago and I cannot escape its hold.

I know it as I think about the meal the entire car ride home. I know it as I close my eyes and all I see is that chicken. I know it as I beg Charles to let me starve the next day and I know it as I take a sleeping pill just so I can get through the night.

ESCAPE

So if anorexia only made me THINK I was in the driver's seat, why did I keep at it? Once I realized that the Eating Disorder had taken over, had drowned out my healthy self, why didn't I fight to get my independence back? I am strong-willed. I am stubborn. Surely, I could regain control easily? For a long time, this type of thinking fueled my self-criticism.

If only it were that simple. Turns out there was a strong part of me that did not want to say goodbye to my ED. Why? Starvation has a numbing effect, while persistent restriction creates a constant distraction. The result? You don't feel anything. You don't have brain space to deal with painful thoughts and emotions. And, to be honest, you are too preoccupied and, eventually too weak, to notice.

I became a robot, simply going through the motions of life but still living. I escaped the ups and downs of the day-to-day. I did not process my anger, pain, resentment or even my joy and happiness. I did not grieve a single loss I experienced. Luckily for me, they were small losses…but they hurt all the same.

When I would try to face my anorexia and start feeding my body, my

emotional freeze would start to thaw. I didn't like that. Not one bit...
because it meant that I started to feel things again. "This isn't fun," I
thought to myself. "The constant battle is exhausting, my digestive
system is all out of whack and these hurtful thoughts are
overwhelming...And, on top of all this, I'm gaining weight in the
process?"

"No bloody way," my mind screamed. "Go back to the good old days
of restriction. Stuff all these feelings and thoughts back down.
Swallow them whole and keep pushing them down deeper until they
are so far down within you that you forget they even exist. I could
literally feel the physical sensation of cramming everything back in
so that I could keep going. It was the only way I knew how to
continue moving.

Eventually, rather than keep pushing everything down, I started
sharing these thoughts, feelings and memories – with my therapist
at first, and then with those closest to me.

These were shameful things – at least to me – and I wanted to bury
them deep within the vault. But, if I couldn't starve anymore, I was
no longer able to keep them locked away.

For years, I had heard that recovery involved accepting thoughts
and allowing yourself to feel. I won't lie, I had no idea how to do that.
I could not understand how to "listen" to myself, to "feel" my feelings.
Impatient with my apparent lack of progress on this front, I became
almost defiant.

"Come on then universe! Bring on the pain, I am ready." And, do you know what happened?

Nothing!

Absolutely nothing. I was trying to force things. Turns out that some things – like feeling – simply cannot be forced. I was ready to give up. I was just going to have to find another way to remain a robot other than starving. Then, one day, I found myself walking the streets of sunny New York when memories I had long suppressed, started coming back to me. This time, I did not push them away. I kept walking and I let them play out before me:

* A perfect December day in London...and the rollercoaster year of loneliness and tears that followed;
* An amazing concert with my best friend...and the lies I told her to avoid recovery;
* Moments of pride...moments of shame;
* The love I felt for my girls...and the thoughts I had of leaving them behind;
* Times I felt valued and appreciated...days I felt taken for granted and invisible;
* Moments I spoke up for those that couldn't...and countless other ones where I allowed people to take advantage of me.

For 2 days, I let this continue and I started to heal...just a little. There is no magical moment in my story where everything was solved. This healing process hurt, but it was also freeing. It was a beginning...less escaping, more living.

Again, allowing myself to feel emotions is not instinctual. For me, it is work. Complicated, hard-to-understand work. I am told that, eventually, when you do it enough, it starts to feel far more natural. It helps you feel a peace that can only come from being truly connected to who you are. Having experienced this a few times now, I believe it.

Activity 4: I Got this Feeling...

When you deny or ignore your emotions, you start to forget what certain things feel like. In my case, I often struggled to understand and explain what I was feeling. When I started to write a food journal, I noticed that I restricted my eating most often when I felt a mix of boredom, wistfulness and sadness. After some meditation and looking though a list of emotions in my group therapy textbook, it hit me. Loneliness! This was my biggest trigger. And now that it had a name, I found it easier to identify it and then challenge myself to stick to my plan when I felt it.

Read through the list of emotions below. During or after a moment that works against your recovery, try to identify what you are/were feeling. Naming your emotion is the first step toward feeling and then... healing.

FEELINGS

Happy

Adored
Alive
Appreciated
Cheerful
Ecstatic
Excited
Grateful
Hopeful
Jolly
Joyful
Loved
Optimistic
Pleased
Satisfied
Tender
Thankful
Uplifted
Warm

Mad

Aggravated
Accused
Angry
Bitter
Defensive
Frustrated
Furious
Hostile
Impatient
Infuriated
Insulted
Offended
Outraged
Rebellious
Resistant
Revengeful
Spiteful
Used
Violated

Sad

Alone
Blue
Burdened
Depressed
Devastated
Disappointed
Discouraged
Grief-stricken
Gloomy
Hopeless
Led down
Lonely
Heartbroken
Melancholy
Miserable
Neglected
Pessimistic
Remorseful
Resentful

Scared

Afraid
Alarmed
Anxious
Cautious
Fearful
Frightened
Horrified
Lost
Haunted
Helpless
Insecure
Nervous
Petrified
Puzzled
Reserved
Tearful
Uncomfortable

Surprised

Astonished
Curious
Delighted
Enchanted
Exhilarated
Incredulous
Inquisitive
Impressed
Mystified
Passionate
Playful
Replenished
Splendid
Shocked
Stunned

Disgusted

Embarrassed
Exposed
Guilty
Ignored
Inadequate
Incompetent
Inhibited
Inept
Inferior
Insignificant
Sick
Shamed
Stupid
Ugly
Unaccepted
Useless

Gladiatorin4inchheels.com

THIS MORNING

I woke up this morning and my stomach was flat. I smiled. I felt strong. I went in the shower and I felt soft flesh on my belly. I did sit-ups to be able to breathe again.

I woke up this morning and my stomach wasn't flat. I was scared and sad. But I smiled and said nothing. I made my girls breakfast and danced as we went to school. I cried as I went to therapy.

I woke up this morning and my clothes were tight. I made Zoe's lunch (macaroni and cheese) and thought about it. I brushed the girls' teeth and thought about it. I dropped the girls off and thought about it. I listened to my stomach rumble and thought about it.

I woke up this morning and you were everywhere – in my dreams, in my shower, in my car. I'm pissed and want to scream: "Fuck off!!! Get out of my head and out of my life. I wish we never crossed paths and I don't want you anymore."

But at the same time, I want to hold on to you, beg you to never leave because you make me feel safe, calm, loved, like I can take on the world. And you have been such an important part of my life that I am scared of what will happen when you are gone. Will I crumble without you? Will everyone see me as I see myself if you are not there to prop me up? I believe most people can understand my reaction of anger. But few can grasp how I can "need" something so destructive. But I do…or at least I think I do – with a conviction more powerful than any other belief I hold.

Currently, there is a storm raging inside me. Me! The person known for seeing sunshine and rainbows in the world. But no one can see it. My weight is up. I have made progress. But with every gram I gain, with every article of clothing I have to retire as too small, my unhappiness grows. I try to deny it, to ignore it, to outrun it.

People look at me and think I am better. And, in some ways I am. So I don't dare share the ticker tape running through my head. If I did, I could only expect them to say what I keep saying to myself: "can't you change the record already?"

Gladiatorin4inchheels.com

I woke up this morning feeling great. I was happy. The sun was shining outside and I sang in the car. I looked in the mirror and liked what I saw. I felt light, energized and free – a glimmer of how I used to feel. I am hopeful and almost don't want to go to sleep, for fear that this moment will slip away.

I woke up this morning, and there you were. I pretended not to see you, ignored your voice. I had let my guard down in the night and you had grabbed hold of me. I dragged you around like a shackle.

I am exhausted but I know this is not the end. I had one day without you. There will be others. I'm doing the hard work. Until then, I sleep the sleep of a battle-scarred warrior – weary, weak...but alert! The wounds will heal. There will be new ones. But the war is not over.

Carry on Gladiator.

THE PLATEAU

I have spent a lot of my recovery in the Plateau. No, not the quaint and hip Montreal borough where parking is scarce while great restaurants abound. Rather, I have spent a lot of time during recovery in the awkward phase between moving forward and stumbling backward.

When I first started to take recovery seriously, I did not deal well with stagnation. I am a doer, a fixer, an achiever. Treading water has never really been my happy place. For a long time, I thought that if I was not moving forward, I was a failure. And if I was unable to recover, I assumed I would be battling anorexia for the rest of my life. As you can imagine, when I felt this stuck, I would ask myself why bother trying to escape the quicksand.

Yup, black and white thinking...a trait of mine, along with many others who battle Eating Disorders and other forms of mental illness.

I spent a very long time in the plateau I call the "Town of Functional Anorexia". It was a place I knew well. After all, I had spent almost a decade there before acknowledging I had a problem. This was largely due to the fact that I didn't see a problem.

I was not anorexic, I was careful with what I ate. I was not anorexic, I was just picky in terms of the taste and texture of certain foods. I couldn't have a problem, I was managing it all. Still, the fact remained that I subconsciously calculated every morsel I ate, oblivious to what I was doing. On the rare occasions that I noticed my controlled consumption, I brushed it off as an infrequent by-product of my anorexic "stint" in my twenties. "I'm just being healthy," I told myself as I turned down the office birthday cake or as I ordered, yet again, the thing on the menu I thought was the best choice rather than the thing I actually wanted to eat.

For an outsider reading my thoughts, it would have been clear that things were "off." But, for me, things were perfectly normal…they were **my** normal. So, I spent very little time concerned about this behaviour, ignorant to the harm I was doing.

Is it true that what you don't know, can't hurt you? Probably not. But, I believe that what you don't know cannot haunt you.

And haunted is exactly how I felt when I plateaued at the functional anorexic phase during my current recovery journey. At this stage, my BMI classified me as underweight, I was still restricting what I ate but ensured I consumed 3 meals a day, and I was accomplishing everything required to do well at work and at home.

Now, you might ask yourself: "what was the problem? You went from crippling anorexia to a functional eating disorder. That is progress. And, after all, you reached a point you had been comfortable with for years. Why the sudden discomfort with being in this place now?"

Ah…but things were different this time. This time, I was acutely aware of where I was. Every disordered thought, every food avoidance became a giant spotlight on my shortcomings. I analyzed my behaviour, chastised myself and compared myself to other periods in my life where I felt I was more invested in recovery. The internal dialogue was non-stop because now I knew what I was doing, what I was tempted to do and I simply could not ignore it. I longed for the past oblivion I had lived in.

During this phase, I became envious of others…no, not of the skinny, not of the rich, and certainly not of the powerful. I was envious of anyone that seemed to confidently eat what they felt like eating, when they were hungry (not starving). I longed to be one of the endless people in a restaurant who simply ordered and ate a meal without it being a "thing". And, while I knew that everyone has issues of their own, I could not see beyond the fact that they were doing a very simple thing that I felt incapable of ever achieving.

I will never forget sitting in my psychiatrist's office, feeling frustrated and unimpressed with my progress. Sure, for a few weeks, I was upbeat, feeling a level of love for myself that I never had before. I was setting daily objectives and meeting them and I had gained weight. But I was seeing myself slip, cutting a corner here and there.

The feeling at the Douglas Eating Disorder Program was that my rate of progress was solid given that I was going it "alone" in outpatient therapy. I heard the words but honestly, I could not see it.

My psychiatrist looked at me and suggested I do more "existing" and less climbing, striving and pushing. I left feeling more frustrated than when I arrived - which was my default reaction to most things those days - but, as with everything, I filed away the message and revisited it periodically until I warmed to the idea and saw what it meant.

I had to stop seeing the plateau as a failure but rather as a necessary step in my recovery. I had to sprint forward and then jog in place for a bit, getting comfortable with where I was and then gather the energy to sprint forward again…and again…and again.

I had learned long ago that recovery could not be a sprint but I had failed to realize that it also could not be a marathon where I moved forward non stop. I had to pause to rest occasionally. And I also had to realize that each sprint forward had to start with small changes and then pick up momentum. If I set the bar too high, I would find it daunting and get discouraged.

I had to stop judging how fast I was making progress and just embrace the fact that I was making progress - however big, however small. I struggled with this concept a lot – particularly because I was ashamed of and discouraged by my stagnation almost as much as by my steps backward. But when I finally started to stop beating myself up over the degree of my progress, it was life-changing.

So when I find myself in the plateau - as I do often - I breathe, and remind myself to focus on the fact that it is a different plateau than the one before, it is closer to my end destination (sometimes by kilometers and other times by centimeters) and that...my friends, is called progress.

Activity 5: Perspective

When you find yourself doubting your progress, ask the people who are closest to you to identify at least one thing that you are doing now to support your recovery that you were not doing before. Odds are that there are many things you have changed that you just don't see. Start each day and end each night reminding yourself of these things.

THE CLIMB

They're everywhere…in my head, on the scale, in my dreams. Lbs, kilos, calories, steps…these numbers are the white noise of my daily life.

Thanks Starbucks for reminding me just how many calories are in that scone I am trying to convince myself to buy and eat (all of it, not a bite or a quarter or a half…the entire 400 calories).

Oh and thanks Fitbit for making it so easy for me to not only track how much energy I expend in a day but to also encourage me to compete with others to see who can walk more in a week.

I am pointing fingers at the tools, but in truth, I don't need them. I can just look at a food item, any item, and guesstimate the caloric content with laser precision. It could be my party trick, I am so good.
Same thing with respect to how active I am. I just know intuitively. Instead of a spidey sense, I have the Peiky ED sense.

And no matter how hard I try – and I have tried, either out of motivation to get well or sheer exhaustion – I cannot turn it off.

The thing about my Eating Disorder is that I use these data points to fuel my competitive nature and try to outperform. And performance is gauged by whatever lens I am using on a given day (healthy or anorexic).

If I am in a healthy/recovery mindset, outperforming involves taking more risks, consuming the same amount of food or more, than the day before. It means being less physically active. It means gaining weight.

But if I am looking at things from my ED perspective, I lower the bar daily with respect to my consumption. It can involve small things like removing a coffee from my routine to removing a food intake from my day. And once you lower the bar, it is extremely difficult to stop yourself from lowering it even further. So it feels nearly impossible to raise it again – unless something dramatic (feeling faint, having heart

palpitations, professional intervention) propels you to action.

Every day is a battle. And a positive trend can turn on a dime, without reason or warning, and you have to find the strength to start the climb again. And it gets harder and harder to lift yourself.

But I do…and then I don't…and then I do.

Recovery is hard. It is not linear and it can be discouraging…for me and, undoubtedly, for everyone that loves me. The disorder can be incomprehensible…even when you are in it, when you feel it, and especially when the numbers swirl around you.

I don't know when or how exactly I will reach the recovered stage. But, I know that when I do, it will be my proudest accomplishment.

So I climb…

GUILT, SHAME AND VULNERABILITY

I feel guilty… a lot. I mean, a lot. It used to be a daily occurrence. Not because I am a horrible person who does horrible things daily and then feels bad about them. On the whole, I feel guilty about almost everything and anything.

I feel guilty if I'm late for work. I feel guilty for going out and missing bedtime. I feel guilty for making a mistake. I feel guilty for forgetting to text a friend on an important day. I feel guilty for needing a break. I feel guilty for spending money and I feel guilty for burning toast. I feel guilty for letting other people down. Essentially, I feel guilty for being human.

The most interesting thing about this guilt is that it is not triggered by others, it is not related to what other people say to me or try to make me feel. Nope. This guilt is entirely created and fueled by me. And, often, it is completely irrational.

For example, I can feel extremely guilty for having a night out even though I know that Charles is a loving and capable parent, who always has everything under control and who never begrudges me for having some time by myself. And yet…

I used to spend a large part of my time away from home thinking about how I SHOULD be home. Ah...I said it... the key word... SHOULD. And who determines what I should be doing? Yup...Me.

I have a lot of ideas that have grown into ideals and expectations of who I am as a person, leader, mother, friend, wife and daughter. And every time I fall short of what I believe I should be doing, I feel an overwhelming sense of guilt. It doesn't even matter to me if the other person notices my behaviour or is impacted by it in any meaningful way. What matters to me is that I noticed. I let myself down.

Sometimes, my guilt was manageable – usually when I was able to justify my "failing". Going out with my girlfriends was ok....as long as I rushed home before my children went to sleep. Having a nap during the day was ok...as long as all the chores were done, the kids didn't need anything, or I was sick.

Sometimes, the guilt brought on by not being who I thought I should be was so strong that it became the most powerful and ugliest force: Shame.

It took me a long time and many instances of butting heads with my therapist to pinpoint the source of this shame. At first, I thought I was ashamed of many things. But, when I boiled it all down, I realized that there was a common denominator: I felt shame when I felt weak.

I was a sensitive child. I cried easily and often. I had separation anxiety. And while my family was fine with it, I soon discovered that the world doesn't always know how to react to tears.

Unconsciously, I began to build my shell and keep things inside. Not crying became another one of my "things" – one of several badges of honor I carried. I became known as the person who never cried at movies and I was incredibly proud of it – so much so that I would swallow any urge to cry when watching something sad simply in order to maintain my image as the strong one, the unfeeling one.

I didn't just deny emotions that made me feel weak; I started denying my needs overall – from my spiritual needs to be loved and understood, to more basic physical needs for rest and, yes, food. I mistook having needs for being needy. I failed to realize that having needs is being human. By trying to override these needs to retain my "power" and rise above, I was trying to suppress my humanity and thus slowly denying who I was as a person, piece by piece.

When I succumbed to my needs, I felt guilt and then shame. Shame, because I had failed to meet the expectations I had for myself. If I went to the spa, I would race home because I felt like a horrible mom for choosing relaxation over my girls. If I ate more than I normally allowed myself to eat, I would berate myself and restrict my eating the next day to make up for giving in to my needs for food. If I stated my needs to my partner, I would panic and fear he would no longer love me and would spend the next few days trying to seek out reassurance that all was ok.

Every time I put myself first, I felt selfish and weak and let the wave of shame wash over me.

If feeling weak brought such strong negative emotions, you can only guess how I saw vulnerability.

For a long time, I saw vulnerability as the greatest form of frailty. I built up a protective wall around my heart and did everything I could to keep up my strong persona. I put on a show. And, when I could no longer deny that I was battling depression and an Eating Disorder, I orchestrated my vulnerability.

I was the master of pretending to be vulnerable without actually opening myself up. It was a clever ruse – I put myself out there, shared the ugly truths of my battle but I did it in an almost flippant way that made it seem like I had everything under control. I wanted to appear strong…struggling but fighting. That way, people would believe I was strong even though, deep down I felt extremely weak.

It worked for a while, until I became so frail – physically and emotionally that all it took was a gentle and compassionate nudge from my best friend, Heather, to let it all out. My network could tell something was going on and Heather sprang into action, booking me for a night out. I had no fight left in me so when she asked how I was doing, I broke down. I told her everything and said I needed help. She sat with me in a Mexican restaurant, as I cried over my salsa, with Mariachi music in the background. She came with me as we went home to finally tell Charles what he already knew: I could not carry on this way anymore.

They both listened to me and came to the hospital 2 days later so that I could seek help. And, while I may have only let go of my need to feel strong because I was too weak to keep it up, I discovered a beautiful secret. Being vulnerable actually is strong and courageous. It involves putting your fears aside and being truly honest about how you really feel and what you really need – regardless of the possible consequences. Being real, after a lifetime of feeling like I had to perform in order to fit the image I had created for myself, was freeing.

I won't lie, being raw and uncensored can be scary and I still sometimes fall into the trap of orchestrated honesty. But, now that I have felt the power of exposing my true feelings and being heard, seen, and understood, it is hard to feel comforted by others when I am wearing a mask.

And, interestingly, I have found that vulnerability can become infectious. When you open yourself up, others do as well, creating closer connections. My husband mirrored my vulnerability and then some. His willingness to share became a catalyst for me to open up even more regardless of how embarrassed I felt.

At one point during my recovery, I was finding it difficult to cope with the stress of juggling work and the healing process. I could feel that I badly needed a mental health day but had to go to Toronto for a networking event. I could not face the trip but could not admit it to anyone, including my husband. So, I lied to everyone. Eventually, months later, I casually mentioned it to Charles, giving it little thought – it felt like it had happened a lifetime ago. He digested the news and openly shared how my inability to be honest with him at the time pained him.

He was right. We were a team and should always be honest with each other. I had forgotten that – something I vow daily to never do again.

His willingness to be open with me about his feelings allowed me to have the courage to start sharing everything I was feeling from that moment on – even if I was ashamed of how I felt or what I had done. No matter how much I judged myself, he didn't.

And, with that, I finally saw that having the courage to be vulnerable with others can inspire them to do the same and create a continuous cycle of honesty and intimacy.

In order to recover and learn to care for myself, I had to change how I viewed both my needs and myself. I had to accept the fact that I am human. Beautifully flawed, but heartwarmingly human.

ACTIVITY 6: Exorcism

Ok, most self-help books ask you to make lists of what you like or dislike about yourself. I'll be honest. I hate these exercises because they are too cerebral. I like to do things, to put myself out there. So, here is an activity designed to help you get some of the shame out of your system. Pick any or all of the following and just let go…

* Find an isolated place outside and scream out the names of all the things that cause you shame

* Take some old dishes, your scale or any other breakable
  objects you don't mind losing. Pick one of these items up,
  name something that causes you to feel shame and break the
  item. Repeat until you run out of sources of shame or
  objects, whichever comes first.

* Write down the things that bring you shame and, either burn
  the list, or leave it in a public place for someone to find.

* Post anonymously on a blog about your shame

* Confide in a stranger on a bus, train, plane, etc (ok, this one is
  ballsy and might require liquid courage but why not try it?)

IF LOOKS COULD KILL

« You look great! », « You look happy », « You seem to be doing well »…

For the average person, hearing these things would be positive, maybe even generate pride – particularly for someone who has been struggling. For me, they are like a kick in the gut. No, not because they trigger anorexic thoughts. Rather, they send me reeling because how I feel is diametrically opposed to how I look.

« Can't you see I am suffering? » I want to scream.   « That I struggle to get through the day? That I still count how many pills I have at home from time to time? …Why can't you see???? »

Depression…it snuck up on me, slowly and quietly as I was working hard on eating again. One day, I was meeting objective after objective, trying new foods and starting to gain weight. The next, a black hood had been placed over my head and I could no longer see my progress, let alone celebrate it.

Fatigue took over, to the point where getting out of bed became a challenge, where standing in the shower seemed like too much work so I switched to baths, where I counted down the hours until my day would end.

Depression started to rob me of feeling. I became numb. I turned into a living and breathing « meh » emoji, sleepwalking through life. I stopped looking forward to things and coasted through the days in a gloomy haze.

This transformation hit me hard. I have long been the energizer bunny. My energy was THE thing that set me apart from others. And now I had to dig deep every day to smile, to lead, to entertain, to pretend. The pressure was high, the shame was intense.

I always viewed my anorexia as a symbol of strength and of self-restraint. And, because that illness was visible to others, I felt a strange sense of peace that my physical appearance matched my inner turmoil.

Not so with depression. Not for me.

What to do?

- • Show up at work in tracksuit bottoms and messy hair to look as rough as I felt?
- • Stop eating so I could start looking gaunt and frail?
- • Put away my trademark shoes and makeup?

No…

I decided to talk about it. Slowly, with my family and close friends, then with a few people I trust at work. And now, on the Blog.

What do I have to be depressed about? Absolutely nothing. I have a great job, 2 amazing and healthy girls, a loving and supportive husband, strong and powerful friendships. What…the…hell?

As someone who has always felt she had to earn everything she has: love, the right to eat, the right to relax, falling prey to depression still does not compute.

And while it is so tempting to deny, to pretend, to hide, I simply don't have the energy to do that.

So instead of spending precious time being ashamed of something that is in no way shameful, I am taking action. I am getting a full checkup this week and am going to give hypnotherapy a try.

Time to find my batteries cause this bunny is intent on coming back.

PERFORMANCE VS PERFECTIONISM

For much of my life, I lumped myself into the category of the perfectionist. After all, I liked to do things right and get top marks, and I shied away from activities where I could not shine. But, I soon discovered that perfection often came at a cost: speed. In addition to its many known downsides, striving for perfection can slow you down...a lot.

And slow, has never been my mode of operation. So, instead, I turned my focus toward performance, achievement, and accomplishment.

Why? Quite simply, perfection does not win as many accolades as consistently completing a large volume of high-quality deliverables. Accomplishing many things extremely well rather than a few perfectly generally impresses and propels you to success – in both life and business. So I made the conscious decision to trade perfection for performance in hopes of outshining others around me.

Still, I never strayed too far from my meticulous roots. My DNA remained largely intact; my distaste for making mistakes remained strong. I had to balance the disappointment related to getting things wrong with the solace brought on by my large volume of completed tasks.

So, I relabeled myself. I was now the Performer – defined by how many balls I could juggle well.

I thought I had it all figured out. The pressure seemed lower than perfection and the recognition I received was more than sufficient. But a dual-pronged problem emerged:

1. I kept upping the achievement ante; and
2. I began to define myself solely by my achiever status.

When I went off work due to anorexia and depression, I was at the height of my career, racking up achievement after achievement. Overnight, I found myself completely devoid of who I believed myself to be.

Well, I couldn't have that. I NEEDED to achieve. If I couldn't get my sense of accomplishment through my work, I quickly and easily turned to my old addiction: restriction. It started off simple enough. The later I waited to eat, the higher the mark I gave myself, the better I felt about who I was. My perceived value was directly measured by my ability to achieve as much as possible, for as long as possible, before I allowed myself to eat. And, every day, I had to match the previous day's performance…no backsliding allowed. In fact, status quo almost felt like a failure.

It didn't matter how I got there, or if I accomplished things perfectly, all that mattered was how long I held on before I gave in to the hunger. This became my metric, my sole source of satisfaction, and I had little energy to care about anything else.

I applied this need to perform to my recovery objectives as well. I made food plans, set daily targets. At first, it was easy. After all, I like making plans and executing them. But, I soon learned this could be dangerous if you try to plan your recovery too far into the future.

Why? Simply because recovery is not... Come on, you know what I am going to say...linear. Recovery is not linear.

From the beginning, the therapists told me this. "Slow and steady," they advised. "You will take steps forward and you will step back; you will rise; and you will fall. Don't plan too far ahead or you might find yourself disappointed when you go off course."

Even though I heard the words, I did not understand them. I couldn't process the fact that my journey would not be a steady climb. Even though I had repeatedly found myself back at the bottom of the mountain, I always thought it would be different the next time – if I really applied myself. So, when I planned way ahead and found myself missing an objective or a target, I took it hard. The disappointment I felt made it more difficult to get back up. And, the more missed targets I faced, the more I was drawn back into the world of restriction. I never missed my restriction targets so it seemed so much more enticing and rewarding to simply focus my energy and efforts on the world of anorexia.

It continued like this until I found myself at the Crisis Center where I had to set and share daily objectives – one therapy goal and one eating goal. No skipping ahead. Objectives were set one day at a time – partially because that is what they asked but also because I was so fragile and deep in my depression and suicidal thoughts that I could not think beyond the day in front of me.

It probably sounds grim but it turned out to be a gift. Initially, I set up a bit of a points system – mirroring the chore chart developed for my girls. To earn points, I had to meet all of my daily objectives. Points could then be accumulated and used for special treats like shoes, spa days, etc.

Setting daily objectives served as a springboard to set longer-term goals. I mostly kept them to weekly goals, with an occasional monthly goal. It worked…until I hit one of my many plateaus and then I could not bring myself to set objectives any more. At the time, I failed to realize 2 things:

1. You don't always have to knock the lights out. Maintaining the status quo can be a very legitimate objective…not forever but for a while at least; and

2. Those pesky doctors were right. Recovery is not linear, and when you find yourself stagnating, going back to daily objectives is not a step backward, it is a way to create the momentum you need to leap forward.

It was hard for my performance-driven nature to accept these things and I still forget them sometimes. But, I am lucky enough to have quite a few people to remind me when I do. It is not just about the target, they suggest. It is also about the many things you learn and accomplish along the way.

Activity 7: Ready, Set, Target

Start small. Go to sleep every night with one objective for the following day. Write it down, email it to yourself, leave yourself a voice mail – whatever works for you. Start each day with this objective in mind. And, because you are not alone, share these objectives with your support network if you feel comfortable. You would be surprised by how much they can help.

I remember in the early days after I started eating, taking pictures of myself achieving certain objectives (eating my morning apple, having a Starbucks muffin, etc) and sharing them with a few select people. Their responses were the boost I needed to push myself a bit more the next day. And, when they knew what I was trying to achieve on any given day, their periodic, pressure-free check-in texts to see how I was doing were exactly what I needed.

PRIORITIES

"Stop for a minute…think about what you just said."

I am sitting in my therapist's office, curled up in a ball with my cow tuque on to keep warm. Uh oh…I think I've just said something "revealing" - something that will lead us to explore further.

I know this is why I dip into my shoe allowance to pay for therapy each week; to be challenged, to be called on my bullshit, to be forced to look at things I would prefer not seeing.

Still, there are times where I wish I had chosen my words a bit more carefully and stayed under the radar.

Ok, Doc, let's do this.

"You just said that writing your blog is the thing you enjoy the most at the moment; why is it the first thing you are thinking of stopping in order to get things done?"

I blink. She blinks right back. This is just one of the numerous times so far in our sessions where I look at her like she is crazy and she waits for me to share what is going on in my head.

Isn't it obvious? It is the least important thing on my list, the one thing that doesn't actually need to be done for life to run smoothly. It is a "luxury".

This leads to an in-depth discussion about why the thing that makes me most happy and fulfilled is the least important to me.

Huh!?

Later in the week, I am faced with a choice: take the shorter route to my destination or the warmer one. Without hesitation, I pick the fastest route. Efficiency over comfort, every time.

As I walk quickly in the freezing cold, it dawns on me. With few exceptions, I continually put efficiency, productivity, work, the well-being of others, etc ahead of my own comfort, needs and well-being.

Gladiatorin4inchheels.com

Why? Because I don't value myself as much as I value others.

I won't pretend to be a saint. I have done things in my life that were epically selfish. In fact, ignorant people might even consider my persistent food restriction despite the harm it causes the people I love to be the ultimate selfish act. I know better...

That said, like many others, I tend to put myself on the bottom of the priorities list simply because I view myself as less important. And this has led to some interesting rules to live by.

For example, my job is to ensure everything is taken care of before I can even consider doing anything else. I can only eat when I've earned it (either by accomplishing tasks or by waiting long enough). I can only miss one bedtime a week. I can only...if...

These are just a few examples of how my lack of self compassion and love manifests itself in my life.

I am not suggesting putting myself above others at all times. It is about balance. About putting the things that make me truly happy and healthy above some of the other things that matter much less in the grand scheme of things.

Let the laundry pile up once in a while, let others sleep at the office in hopes of getting the promotion, tell my kids no once in a while...
All so I can dance and sing with abandon, do some of the things I love, eat when I am hungry, listen to myself.

And keep blogging.

NO ONE CAN SAVE YOU BUT THEY CAN HELP

When I started to truly open up to others I realized just how many people around me could help. I knew many of them wanted to offer support but didn't know how and I honestly didn't think they would be able to. How could they help me when the issue stemmed from the wiring in my brain?

"Just eat", "think of your girls", "we love you", I heard all of these things and was convinced that no one could help me - not my family, not my friends, not my doctors. At first, I pushed all of these people away, telling myself I was going to have to tackle this all on my own. I retreated from others, I skipped therapy, I read books, I made plans, and I pretended I had it all under control.

It worked for a while until my brain decided that restriction and anorexia were the only things that could help. I felt lost. I started to wait for that one person who would understand everything, who had the magic potion to fix it all. I was waiting to be saved. I was the clichéd damsel in distress, hoping that if I got sicker, somehow it would bring on my salvation.

On these occasions, I would spiral until I hit a real low, forcing me to pursue some kind of treatment. And then the cycle would continue all over again.

It wasn't until I found myself being refused admittance to the psych ward at a local hospital that I had to admit what I was doing. The psychiatrist looked me in the eye, as I stared back through tears and anger and said:

"Admitting you will not give you what you need. You are looking for us to lock you up and save you. It doesn't work that way. You will only wind up feeling a whole lot worse. No one can save you, Christina. You have to save yourself by being patient, doing the work and letting others in to help you."

At first, I was furious. But, when my anger had subsided and I had cried beyond the point of exhaustion, I started to do just that. What choice did I have?

I started at the Crisis Center, where I openly shared my struggles with the people living with me. This may seem like a no-brainer but for me, it was a huge step. I would normally have kept things to myself because my suffering seemed to pale in comparison to their stories. The old me would have felt I was surrounded by people who outranked me in the pain department. I would have been too shy and ashamed to share my story out of fear of being judged as a wimp. I could just imagine them thinking: "That's it? You are here because you want to die cause you are afraid of food? Food!!!"

But, as these people opened up and shared their stories with me, all

I could do in return was tell my own.

I realized that I did not have to be the person with the worst problems to be able to admit to and share my own struggles. So I talked…and they listened…and they cheered when I ate the dinner we made instead of opting for toast. It was this experience, feeling the compassion and support from people who were facing rather large challenges in life that propelled me forward.

Every day at the Center, I felt stronger and bolder. I started by taking a walk and having a bagel at Tim Horton's – something I had not done in almost a year. Fueled by that, I went for breakfast the next morning at Première Moisson AND had lunch with Charles AND then dinner. 3 full meals in one day…this was big. These small, but big steps, lead me to do something I never thought I would do: I decided to leave all of the "skinny clothes" I had brought with me at the Crisis Center when I left. It was a symbolic move, really, because I could always go buy some more. But, for me, it was a commitment to myself that I was leaving a part of me behind.

As I left the Center, I picked up some new items for my wardrobe in a size bigger. Six months later, I have not gone down a size and, if I come across an item of clothing on the smaller side, I throw it out so that I am not tempted to shrink my frame.

While I discovered the power of having a network at the Crisis Center, the feeling was cemented in my life when I got out, where Charles and I spent many late nights talking by the fire. I am convinced that these chats saved my life. When I first came home, we talked every night until my body cried for sleep. We shared everything we had held inside for so long – things like how we saw a gap form between us after the children were born but did not know how to change things; or how we stopped appreciating each other.

We asked questions we had longed to ask but didn't for fear of upsetting the other person – Charles asked where my libido went (answer: antidepressants); I asked why it mattered to him (answer: he showed and felt love through touch; He asked why it didn't matter to me (answer: I show and feel love through words). Ah...

We saw each other in a way we had not been able to do before. We developed a new level of intimacy because we now had an even greater understanding of our shared reality. And, we knew what made each other tick. For example, when I am struggling or feel hurt, my tendency is to withdraw. When I do that, Charles feels excluded...this is not a good recipe for mutual support.

Having shared these reactions, we are now better able to understand each other and address things head on. If I retreat, Charles asks me what's up. If I am struggling, instead of retreating, I do my best to be honest. In some cases, it is as simple as saying: "I am having a hard time right now. I am not ready to talk about it but I promise I will. I just need x (in some cases it is to have a bath, in others, it is to skip the bacon in my sandwich, etc). Either way, it brings Charles in rather than leaving him out.

And, it wasn't just my romantic relationship that grew stronger. In time, I also opened up to my team at work – who encouraged me and praised me as I started to bring in breakfast and hot lunches. And with my friends, who encouraged me to take calculated risks.

Everyone I told seem to respond with kindness and support. I thought that since the illness was so misunderstood, they would stereotype and say the wrong thing. But, they didn't need to understand anorexia to help me, I realized. All I needed were people to notice me, my actions, my moods and say a few words to help keep me going.

Huh!

No matter the kind of relationship – romantic, family, friend – wherever possible try not to run away. Don't shut people out. And remember, you don't have to bare your soul to let people in. You just have to remain present and share a minimum level of your own truth.

As I started to fuel my body, my brain and my spirit, a new kind of clarity emerged when I looked at my life. I began to see some of the other negative influences around me. While it was hard, I had to walk away from certain things in order to truly work on recovery. It meant leaving some fair-weather friends behind and limiting the negative self-talk I seemed to love so much.

After a few months, as I adapted to my new life, I was able to invest more and more in my recovery. My weight started to climb a little bit – moving me out of the danger zone – and stayed there.

But ups and downs are standard in this type of recovery so all was not rosy every day. There were times where I struggled with my objectives or with my emotions. Immediately, my instinct was to withdraw and restrict. I could physically feel myself detach from the world around me.

And this is where my network really helped. Knowing what to look for, Charles would draw me back. My friends too would check in with each other to gauge how I was doing. My colleagues checked to see if I ate and reminded me how much I loved my Starbucks muffin. And, I started to develop ways to prevent my desire to run away every time I felt wounded.

Some of these coping mechanisms might surprise you.

Say what you want about Facebook, the memories, pictures and videos it houses were a real lifeline for me at times. Reliving happy memories that popped up in my feed helped me smile most days and reminded me that there is good in the world and in my life.

I know I am lucky. Not everyone has a strong circle of family, friends and colleagues to support their recovery. I know that.

But, I also know you don't need to have an army surrounding you. It just takes one person…one person for you to open up to, who can respond to your pain with compassion and remind you that you are not alone.

Activity 8: Someone

Think about the people in your life. It can be a long list or a short one. It can consist of people you know well or people who know very little about you. There is no complex criteria. All you need is one person who is present in your life – it can be a partner, a friend, a parent, a doctor, a neighbor, the mailman…it doesn't matter.

Just pick one person and tell them, genuinely, how you are doing. If it is a great day for you, tell them. Say: "I am having a really great day today." If it is the opposite, say so. Odds are, they will respond, and when they do, share as much with them as you feel comfortable. Share as much as you feel like sharing. It might not be much on one day. You may just admit that you are having a tough time and leave it at that. Or, you might reveal more.

The key here is to do it and then keep doing it until you find yourself at a point where you share more and more of yourself, of your feelings and of your battle. This can be extremely powerful.

I remember finding myself crying outside of the office one day, trying to pretend I was fine and a stranger came up to me and said: "It will get better." I nodded and agreed even if I wasn't sure he was right.

Still… it made all the difference.

So, go on…give it a try. Tell me…how are you today?

BADASS

"You're a badass...

I am no stranger to therapy. And, one of the things I hear a lot in my sessions is the importance of letting go and "listening" to the universe, a higher power, God, or whatever you want to call it.

I'll admit to a certain amount of skepticism about this universe business. But, recently, I've been finding myself thinking about it a lot.

A few weeks ago, I was feeling unsure of myself. I went onto my iPad to write a blog and the first words I saw were: "You're a badass."

My first reaction was to stop and agree with the statement. Yes, yes I am. And, while I agreed with the words, they seemed to come out of nowhere – until I remembered it is the title of a book someone recommended.

That entire day, I felt badass. I was confident, I was happy and I was strong. Maybe it was a pure coincidence. Maybe not. But whatever it was, it changed the entire dynamic of my day.

Hmmm...

When I started the coaching program, I was afraid. After almost a year of being off work, much of which was spent in a haze of deprivation, and after a failed attempt to return to work, I was unsure I could cope mentally with the course load.

On the first day, I skipped breakfast so was feeling a bit weak and particularly doubtful about my abilities. I was lost in negative thoughts when the professor – almost as though she was reading my thoughts – broke my reverie by saying: "each of you is a fascinating individual and we were thoroughly impressed by your applications, your wealth of experience and backgrounds. If we didn't think you should be here, we would not have selected you to be part of the program."

Hmmm again.

Gladiatorin4inchheels.com

Now, I can't say that I've been converted into a very spiritual person. I tend to skim the higher power sections in the various self-help books I read. But, I have to admit that there may be some truth to the notion that being more present allows us to hear messages we may have ignored before.

I've been encouraged to get more in touch with who I am, what I need, etc. My response has always been, sure thing, what is the step-by-step process to do that. Apparently, it doesn't work that way. I need to slow down...listen...wait...listen...wait some more...

Ok! I sit down, put on some music, breathe and just wait...Nothing....I'm so frustrated with myself...I cannot hear anything. No inner voice, no inner child...Maybe I'm broken....I have nothing to tell myself...All I hear is my stomach grumbling....

Oh...

Hello body; hello hunger. It has been a while since I allowed myself to hear you. Maybe I'll start with listening to you and see what happens....

FALLING IN LOVE

I'm a hard person to love. I say this not because people have told me this and not because past friends or lovers have cut me out of their lives – though some have. I say this because much of my recovery has centered around me learning to love and accept myself.

I was a textbook case of a person who could not make herself a priority. Somewhere along the way, I lost sight of every person's birthright – the right to be loved and to love unconditionally. For various reasons, over the course of my life, I started to believe that love had to be earned – you had to be selfless, get good grades, stay out of trouble, keep the peace...

Earning it once did not mean it could not be taken away at any given moment. So, I had to keep earning. And, eventually, I made it a daily quest to earn and maintain the love of others. When I had kids, it became worse. Even though I knew there was nothing that could ever change how much I loved my girls, I was afraid that they would turn their backs on me if I was less than perfect. I was convinced that I would lose their love, respect and admiration, if I strayed from the cardboard cutout I designed for myself. The same thinking applied to my friends and colleagues.

All this to say I was a bit lacking in the self-love department. Turns out I was not the only one. I soon discovered a myriad of books on the matter.

For over a year, I read a lot, saw several therapists, desperately looking for the step-by-step process I needed to follow to fall in love with myself.

Hmmm. No one seemed to have the answer. Even the people that loved me could not show me the way. I started to think that this self-love business was a load of BS – the thing people pointed to when they were not quite sure what would help. You know, kind of like when doctors aren't quite sure what you have so they say it is a virus. It felt like an easy "out."

I was ready to give up on it all. Then I found a book that changed my life and this love yourself business started to make sense.

I was skeptical from page 1 but I had nothing left to lose so I kept reading, kept completing the exercises. And, while I cannot say for sure if it was the book or my strong desire to change or both but I started to feel things start to shift.

The biggest gift this book provided was the concept of a mantra…a sentence I repeated daily to give me a boost. I said it in the shower, I said it as I walked into the office and I said it to calm my anxiety. If I felt stressed at work, in moments of self-doubt, I would leave my desk and go for a short walk and simply repeat the following words: "I love myself." Doing this helped in many ways. It changed my anxious mind track, it calmed me down and it allowed me to take a step back from the situation.

I was less impulsive as a result and started to make better decisions.

In time, I evolved this concept to something that worked even better. Always a big fan of music as a background to life, I replaced my mantra with a theme song. The song varied daily but I remember walking into the office listening to Confident by Demi Lovato and feeling invincible. I remember another time walking on a country road in the rain, smiling, carefree and singing along to Paula Cole's Me.

Not your type of songs? No problem. Find your own and go to your happy place.

I started to see a difference in people's reactions to me as well. I started to receive more random compliments from strangers on the street. Colleagues seemed to give more heed to what I had to say.

I chose to accept these positive affirmations even if I did not believe what was being said. In the past, when I received compliments, I tended to downplay them or downright contradict them in my mind, pushing away the positive view others had in favor of the negative one I had of myself. Now, even if I still don't believe everything I hear, I just accept the words as gifts – some I put on the shelf, and some I embrace straightaway. And, surprise, it helps.

Oh…and…I smile! I try to smile at the beautiful things I see and hear

– sunshine, kids laughing, champagne, my children sleeping, theme parks, the beach, leaves changing, I could go on. The world is a beautiful place.

The last thing, and the most difficult one for me, was learning to listen to myself and giving myself permission to meet my needs. The somewhat insurmountable task here was actually knowing what I needed. On this point, my therapists were quite helpful. They were patient but relentless, asking me questions to help me connect to who I was. Often, I had no answers. I had such a strong disconnect between who I really was versus the image I had conjured of myself. This disconnect remains extremely strong and I have recently started hypnotherapy to bridge the gap. But, I will say this, every once in a while, a thought pops up that tells me what I want and I no longer push it away.

For example, I often found myself doing things out of a sense of obligation, out of a feeling of "I should" – particularly with social outings. In my new job, socializing is a big part of the culture. And, I would often have to force myself to go to these things…or worse organize them! Sure, let's ask the anorexic to pick the menu for our cocktail…sigh. Often, I would dread the whole thing, grin and bear it but not really interact with others – defeating the whole purpose of attending.

Now, I limit the number of activities I attend and have explained to my colleagues that I am happy to connect in many different ways but I need to limit them in order to maintain my balance with my home life. I also explain that food cannot be at the center of these activities because, while I am in recovery, food can still trigger my anxiety and old habits. It took me a while to feel comfortable enough to say this to my colleagues but at least then they understood the reasons behind my avoidance and did not take my actions personally.

Speaking your truth and living it can be powerful.

All this is great but there are days where I still struggle to find my smile and where listening to my current theme song on continuous loop just doesn't cut it. On those days, I don't force it. I just go on autopilot for a bit, going through the self-love motions and then find myself back to the place where my MOJO is strong.

ACTIVITY 9: Change your Lens

One of the things I kept hearing from my friends during my darkest days was that they wished I could see myself as they saw me. So, for my 40th birthday, I asked some of them to share drawings of how they saw me. What came in was touching, funny and beautiful.

For this activity, draw a picture of yourself. Ask others to draw what they see and share it with you. Ideally, do this as a group activity so that you can all share, laugh, cry and drink some wine. Keep these drawings close – maybe keep a picture of them on your phone – and look back on them every once in a while to remember that you are a wonderfully complex person whose beauty is defined differently by those around you.

ME

"It is 9:30 pm. I'm sitting in bed with both girls sleeping beside me, the glow of my iPhone is the only thing lighting up the room. I type a message to Charles and hit send:

"I cannot do this anymore."

After an hour of whining, cajoling, arguing, bribing, punishing, capitulating and begging, the girls are finally asleep. Recently, the bedtime routine has been more difficult. The girls are more resistant to everything and they shun their father completely, leaving me with the difficult challenge of being fully present when they want to tell me about their day, just moments after having been the authoritarian mom. I usually feel so mentally and physically drained by the end of it that it is not unusual for me to fall asleep as they drift off for the night. Tonight was especially difficult. There were frustrated voices and tears…mine included.

So, I type…and send my cry for help. It is well received and a solution is found for the next night.

With 2 kids under the age of 7, these situations are bound to happen. They've happened before and they will surely re-occur. But I have changed the way I handle them.

18 months ago, when I would feel overwhelmed and overworked at home, I would say nothing. It was my job after all…they were asking for me, they needed me. I kept everything inside, felt like I was failing as a mom and my frustration built – eventually coming out in passive aggressive behaviour…ok sometimes aggressive aggressive behaviour.

A year ago, I started to share when I was feeling this way. But I struggled with how to say I was struggling. It sometimes came out all wrong and, often, no matter how I shared how I was feeling, I did nothing to help myself. Sometimes I downright resisted offers of help.

Gladiatorin4inchheels.com

Why? Well, because the overwhelmed feeling passed and I wanted to power through and be there for my kids when they wanted me. I told myself that all I needed was a good night's sleep and I would reboot.

A good idea in theory but it was not always the case. Sometimes, I would get so close to my maximum threshold that even a good night's sleep would only do so much.

This week, I not only sent out the SOS but I took action to help myself. Deep down, I knew I needed a night off from bedtime. And I took it. I kissed the girls goodnight and left them with their loving dad even though they begged me earlier in the day not to leave.

I went to my parents' house, snuggled up in a blanket with a cup of coffee and read in complete silence, with no threat of interruption. When they were sleeping, I made my way home.

Some might find this a bit of an odd action. And maybe it was. I know I felt a bit embarrassed that I had to leave the house. But, for me, it was an important step in self care. I did what I had to do to give myself some time, even though I felt guilty about it at first. And putting my needs ahead of guilt is progress.

This is imperfect me…growing.

GO FOR GREY

If I had a nickel for every time I heard about Black and White thinking in therapy, I would be able to retire…easily. It got to a point that I would roll my eyes. But as with most things that we judge, I simply didn't understand the concept.

I saw myself as a measured and balanced person who never thought in extremes. But this perception was flawed and based on a filtered interpretation of myself. I ignored all the times I discarded people or things that didn't fit perfectly with how I thought they should be. I even forgot my panicked reaction to when I became ill. "I can't be sick, I'll have to leave my new job, disrupt my finances and my life. It will be horrible. So, just pretend everything is ok, you don't need help. Pretending is the only alternative to seeking help."

Pretending is the only alternative…if I had to pay a nickel for every time I thought that, I would have to work 2 lifetimes.

Breaking through the all-or-nothing way of thinking is one of my ongoing challenges. If someone doesn't react the way I expect them to, I am strongly tempted to cut them off. If things aren't going well at work, I immediately think about finding a new job. I don't always follow through with these thoughts but they are indicative of my propensity to see and operate in a world of black and white.

I am working hard on discovering the shades of grey in life. It is a gradual thing and it is very much a work in progress. But I have come to learn that sometimes, the greatest source of progress is discovering and embracing the grey.

The day before the day I started eating was the day where I stumbled upon the grey. If you recall, I had just been denied admission at the psychiatric ward at the hospital. I was desperate because I thought that meant my only alternatives were to pretend everything was fine or go back on the Douglas waiting list for in-patient therapy. Then, I discovered the Crisis Center. Grey!

The Crisis Center presented an option that allowed me to seek help without going off work…again. It allowed me to re-center, re-focus and build the strength I needed to start the hard climb all over again. It was my first taste of grey and it made a big difference in my recovery. It was motivating and empowering. And it taught me to pause when I was examining alternatives in order to see if there was a third alternative to my automatic all-or-nothing way of thinking.

A key part of the recovery process is to continually ask yourself if there is another perspective you haven't considered. For example, I no longer think that if I am not showing clear signs of improvement health-wise, it means I am deteriorating. Not gaining weight doesn't necessarily mean I am taking a step back and destined to wind up where I started.

Restricting a few days doesn't mean that recovery is hopeless and I should give up. Having a bad day at work doesn't mean I've lost my edge. Eating more than I usually allow myself to eat one day doesn't mean I have to punish myself the next day to compensate. Being impatient with my girls one moment doesn't make me a horrible mother. Gaining weight doesn't mean I am getting fat. Eating more doesn't mean I will never be able to stop. Getting lost does not mean that I cannot be found.

Sideswiping another car doesn't make me a bad driver....wait... actually, that one is true in my case!

You get the point, thinking in extremes limits you and can be a big source of dissatisfaction, guilt and misplaced shame.

You may be reading this and thinking that might work for others but it won't for you. Trust me, it can...it won't always work but that does not mean you should throw the concept way. They key word is it **can**. It doesn't mean it is a given or that it will always work. But it could, so try to remain open to the possibility...and therein lies the grey.

Activity 10: In Between

I am a firm believer in starting small to move to the big. And, sometimes looking at past examples can help coach your brain to start seeing things differently in the present.

So, identify 3 examples from your past where you thought in extremes. Draw a line with 2 poles. Put the extremes for each example on either pole. Now, think....see how many options you can identify in between the poles.

For example:

Let's say you went out to dinner and ate more than you typically allow yourself to eat, indulging in a dessert and a drink or two. You wake up the next morning feeling physically full and anxious. You have two thoughts:

> * I went overboard last night, I must eat as little as possible today to reset.

> * I indulged, lost control, what is the point, I might as well keep overindulging today.

Full

restriction_____Overeating

See if you can identify other options between the two.

This is just an example, you can use any situation where you saw only two alternatives. You don't have to find many options in between. The key here is to find at least one and to train your brain to pause during your decision-making and see if you can identify at least one other solution to every dilemma you face.

Not working? Try it another way. Take the same example but imagine that the person in the situation is not you but a friend. Now, can you identify other alternatives. Sometimes, taking yourself out of the equation helps see new ways of doing things.

FUNHOUSE

"Life with an eating disorder (ED) is very much like being in a fun house. You live in a perpetual state of distortion: physical, emotional and cognitive.

Body image distortions are typical of someone with an ED. It can happen when you look in the mirror; you see chubby when others see bone. It can happen when you look at yourself in pictures. It can happen when you are in the shower or getting dressed and you feel a little extra flesh.

To be honest, it can even happen when you look at others. Either you see them as thinner than they are and you are envious; or you see them as bigger than they truly are.

One of the hardest things for me during recovery has been feeling my body changing – feeling soft flesh where I used to feel taught skin. Even though my weight gain has been relatively small compared to my first recovery 10 years ago, I mourn the loss of my angular body daily.

I curse the curves I feel appearing. I look at pictures of myself when I was at a healthy weight and I think: big. I didn't at the time, but now I do. And even though I can see the nonsense of it all, I cannot seem to find the right lens to look through. And, unfortunately, until I do, I live my days pushing away the unease I feel with how I look, knowing that I have to keep eating while desperately hoping my vision corrects itself soon.

Then there are the emotional distortions. As an insecure, conflict-avoiding overachiever, I've long developed a habit of keeping negative thoughts and feelings inside, pushing them away, swallowing them whole. Doing this has been my way of avoiding certain feelings and thoughts, and generally from dealing with s**t. Just keep swimming, Peiky. Don't think; don't feel; just…keep…swimming.

I've found that if you do this enough, without realizing it, you become numb, out of touch with who you are, what you want and how you feel.

Gladiatorin4inchheels.com

For example, I felt angry when I was really hurt, restless when I was really lonely and anxious when I was actually afraid. I'm still untangling all this but I have recently expanded my emotional vocabulary from the 5 emotions featured in the film Inside Out (anger, joy, fear, disgust and sadness) to well over 25 different feelings. Take that Pixar!

Then we enter the chamber of cognitive distortions. These are the most damaging in my opinion because they can be deeply rooted in your psyche and span all areas of your mind.

While I've fallen victim to several of these, **Black or White** thinking is one of my "favorites". Miss a meal, the day is a right-off so why bother trying; have a tough time at work, time to find a new job; someone hurts your feelings, they don't care about you so cut them out; hit another car, you shouldn't be driving…well… maybe that one is more a reality than a distortion. (Is this driving humor getting old? Cause I could go on forever)

I'm also great at overgeneralizing. I have fat, so I am fat. I was impatient with my girls, I am a horrible mother; I went on sick leave, I'm weak, washed up and no one will want me.

These are all thoughts I've had but know deep down are untrue. Still, when you live in the funhouse, you sometimes forget what is real. You need to be strong to keep your eyes and your mind in focus. Some days are more successful than others.

So, I continue my way toward the exit of this house of mirrors I made for myself. I know it will take time and I will take a wrong turn here or there. But, when I do find my way out, I will not leave empty-handed. I will be wiser, more confident, more relaxed about the things I cannot control (which, let's be honest, is a lot)…

Oh! And I'm totally bringing the mirror that makes me look 6ft tall as a memento.

MAMMA

"Just try it, please…One bite…please!"

Nope…I am not trying to get my girls to eat broccoli – they both
actually like it.

Rather, it is Zoe asking me to try something I don't normally eat. Today,
I am lucky. She is offering me cheese, something I've never loved but
that I still consider edible. Some days, particularly if we are out for Dim
Sum, her offerings have me backing away, shaking my head, jaw
locked.

What kind of message am I sending to my impressionable girls?
Hmmm…

From the moment you decide to become a parent, you start to worry.
You worry about getting pregnant. You worry about making it to end of
the first trimester. You worry about what you eat, how much you sleep,
the level of stress in your life. You worry about the birth and, then…
well… then you really start to worry. I'm told this never ends, no matter
how old your children are. As a mom, I am certainly no stranger to the
big "W."

As a parent living with anorexia and raising 2 young girls (Zoe is 7 and Lily is 5), I have a whole different level of concerns.is 7 and Lily is 5), I have a whole different level of concerns.

Research has shown that Eating Disorders are caused by biological, psychological and social factors.

Evidence suggests that some people are genetically predisposed to developing an Eating Disorder. Some literature predicts that someone with an anorexic mother is 12 times more likely than someone with no family history to develop it themselves (Eating Disorders Review, Nov/Dec 2002).

The first time I heard this, I started to panic. My girls! My genes! My anxiety!! Luckily my therapist was there to remind me of a few important things. First, while my girls share some of my DNA, their genetic makeup is not identical to mine. Second, being genetically predisposed to an Eating Disorder does not mean you will fall prey to its insidious grasp. Other factors need to come into play to help trigger the ED.

Ok, so no need to panic right away…but…wait…what are the other factors, again?

Certain psychological traits tend to be common among people with Eating Disorders. Perfectionism, feelings of inadequacy, having a poor sense of self, and seeing the world as black and white are typically exhibited by ED sufferers. Sound familiar?

Then there are the social factors. The beauty messages that are pervasive in our modern society. Body image messaging (positive/negative, spoken/implicit) is everywhere. And it is not just in Hollywood or on social media. It is much much closer to home: in the school yard, at family gatherings, even with friends. And, of course, in my own kitchen. So I spend my days on high alert, intent on teaching my daughters a healthy way to live.

In arming my girls against an ED, my focus has been on reducing the social factors that can contribute to an Eating Disorder. I tell them they are beautiful and to never let anyone tell them otherwise. I compliment them on all aspects of their beauty, not just the physical: their sense of humour, kind hearts, intelligence, generosity, determination – and I tell them every day that they are wonderful and magical.

Knowing there is nothing lonelier than keeping parts of yourself hidden, I encourage my girls to share their thoughts and feelings, to express who they are freely, to share their needs.

With respect to food, the message is simple. Eat when you are hungry; stop, when you are full. Nothing is forbidden for them – though I do teach them moderation and that it is important to be mindful about wasting food. I align their portions to what Charles gives them. No longer do they have toast with the thinnest layer of peanut butter or homemade pizza with a few sprinkles of cheese. They must have thought I was rationing their food.

Still, no matter what I say or how I feed them, the girls see my sparse portions, they know I have forbidden foods and they see things on their plates that I, myself, am too picky to try.

And, they pick up on everything. Recently, Zoe gave me a nickname: "Gummy." I had no idea where this came from and she could not explain it. This continued for months without me thinking anything of it – until my sister came for a visit and quickly figured it out. "Um…Christina, when your daughter calls you Gummy because you chew a lot of gum instead of eating, maybe you aren't fully recovered?" Oh…

As parents, Charles and I have tried our best to counter the mixed messages I send by being clear about who is the exception and who is the rule. My daughters know that I am not the example to follow when it comes to eating. And they know I am the one who has work to do. Still, I am never sure if these messages have truly sunk in. I wonder if they will continue to do as I say and not as I do as they grow up.

There are signs of hope. Just as I was wondering if they understand that I have a disorder, Zoe announced to the family last Christmas Eve: "You're not healthy mommy! You don't eat enough." Ok, maybe it is sinking in a bit. Please let it sink in more.

So, on the whole, we are managing these tricky waters. The hardest phase we have gone through together so far was during my treatment at the Douglas. .

When I went off work and started seeing many doctors, my wee ones became extremely clingy and tried whatever excuse they could find to stay home. School drop offs were more difficult. Lily would go to bed every night begging me not to go to daycare the next day. And, while they never said it, I believe they were scared that I was really sick. I tried to explain my health issues in ways they could understand ("the doctors are helping mommy eat more") and reassure them ("I'm not going anywhere").

I even involved them in making a sticker board to track my food intakes (6 intakes per day gets you a sticker). We talked about it often and, when I shared with them my disappointment around having to leave the Douglas early, Zoe hugged me and told me she loved me, even if I "failed food school."

Since I have begun eating more, I remind them again and again that I am still not setting the example to follow – especially on days when I remain empty-handed at our Dairy Queen outing. Still, I know the risk for them to fall into unhealthy patterns remains and will continue until I am fully recovered.

So, I watch for signs, I tell them they are beautiful and I try very hard not to say or do anything that will harm them…oh…and I pray. And as much as I try to teach them, I also let them teach me. They have many lessons to bring. Here are just a few:

* Laugh...ok, so they fight, they whine, they get angry, but our household is filled with laughter most of the time. The best laughter of all – deep belly-cramp giggles that are infectious and that make you smile when you hear them. The kind you would like to record and have as your daily soundtrack.

* Forgive...there are times when the forgiveness starts more as a parental request. But young children generally do not bear grudges. They seem better at separating the act from the person.

* Embrace who you are. The other day, Zoe looked at herself in the mirror and said: "I'm fabulous" just as Lily ran through the house naked asking me to look at her big, big belly, beaming with pride. Really, need I say more about this? I wish we all kept this level of unblemished self-confidence, this lack of questioning ourselves and just knowing deep within our souls how wonderful we are.

Activity 11: A Day in the Life

As part of the nighttime routine in your household, get as close to your kids as they will allow – depending on the age, it can range from cuddling to simply allowing you to be in the same room as them.

Ask your kids to share with you the best part of their day. You might be surprised at what you learn about them and, in some cases, about how important you are to them. My girls are fairly young and perhaps this colors their perception, but I found that, often, the best part of their day involved being with mom.

Share the best part of your day with them as well. Again, you may find yourself realizing that your best moment is in fact a mom moment.

Do the same after that with the least favorite part of your day. This will encourage your children to open up – not only about the good aspects of their daily lives but also about the harder parts – teaching them the power of vulnerability.

If they are aware of your Eating Disorder, this is an opportunity to share with them your ups and downs – to the extent you feel is healthy and valuable to them.

BAD MOMMY

"You're a bad mommy."

I used to hear these words a lot...like a lot. And every time they were said to me, I felt a little smaller (not good in general, worse when you are 4 ft, 11 and a half inches tall); my world lost a little bit of color. The bizarre thing is that my girls never said these word to me. I did.

Perfectionism is sometimes painted as a positive. We associate it with being driven, with quality and with commitment. But for some, the desire to be perfect is so strong that they miss out on life – either refusing to try anything they are not good at or simply spending all of their time looking for points to take off of their scorecard. The constant quest for 100% takes a lot of fun out of the game.

In some areas, where being perfect matters less to me because it seems impossible to achieve, I use humour to deal with my disappointment. I laugh about my height, my bad driving skills, my horrible cooking abilities (her father is a chef!!!) as a coping mechanism.

Now, when perfection matters most to me – work, my career, being a good mom – I am unforgiving. If I feel my performance is stellar, I am on the highest of highs. Achievement fuels me like nothing else. But when I fall short of my expectations, my self-esteem takes a hit. Over the years, I've developed many tools to help ensure a solid report card at work. Long hours, great mentors, a strong network, good bosses (minus one or two) and rock star team members have been my safety nets. If I felt out of my depth, I could always count on anorexia to help me gain my sense of power and control to turn things around.

As a mom, I felt much more unsteady and the stakes were higher. Screw up and you potentially screw up your child. Ok, I am being a bit dramatic but the pressure I put on myself was high. In my mind, I had to be ever-patient, loving and entertaining; part child psychologist, rule maker, nurse, teacher, encyclopedia...all while smiling, keeping everything up at work and wearing heels.

I worried constantly about my mistakes, read articles about parenting. If I lost it during the morning school run, I spent the drive into work replaying the incident and vowing to be better next time.

Gladiatorin4inchheels.com

I cannot even talk about the bedtime routine! I started getting up at 5 am so I could work out before the girls woke up. I didn't want to eat into any mommy/girls time.

Being a mom started to feel like a job I was inadequate at. I would look at the moms on the playground laughing and totally focused on their kids. There I was, half paying attention to the girls, typing away on my blackberry and wondering what "chip" I was missing.

Don't get me wrong. In the midst of all this, I knew I loved these girls with all that I am and all that I have. Without question, they are the best thing in my life. But, I felt I was missing the mommy "secret sauce."
It was about this time that my world came crashing down. As I started to dig out of the rubble, a few things happened.

I started to slow down and see things more clearly as opposed to a blur of activity and negative self-talk. I saw more beauty in the world.

I discovered self-compassion and noticed things I liked about myself. And slowly, when I looked in the mirror, I saw me again. A person. Flawed but beautiful – as each and every one of us is…human.

I started being open and honest with the girls when I felt overwhelmed or when I felt I messed up. Turns out, they are far more forgiving than I ever was with myself and they think I am the best mom. I see it in their faces when I pick them up at the end of the day and feel it in every hug and kiss.

I saw my girls in a new light. I started to connect with them more; to share my learnings, to stop and really listen to them. And, oh, how I fell even more in love with them.

It is not always easy and I am by no means any closer to being a perfect mom. (If anyone knows one, though, please send her my way so she can babysit.) But I am coping with this fact in a much healthier way and I'm not sure how I know this, but deep down I know I am a good mom.

Am I silly mommy; a song and dance mommy; a loving mommy; an imperfect mommy; a sometimes embarrassing mommy (just wait for the teen years)? You bet.

But am I a bad mommy? No fucking way.

EMBRACING YOUR SUPER HERO

I was never a big Marvel Comics kind of person. In fact, I was an Archie fan. All those high school antics and love triangles. But, throughout my life, a few Superheroes have left an impression. Superman, Batman, they were cool. Spider-man, meh. Thor...well, there is a certain appeal as you get older. But, when I was a girl, no one could compare to Wonder Woman.

As we often do as we grow up, I forgot about her until recently. And, it didn't take long before she became my hero all over again. Strong, confident, badass...a mix of beauty, strength and intelligence. I cannot think of a better role model. As I battled through my own personal struggles, she became my inspiration. She is the screensaver on my phone and she is the image I channel when I need strength.

Heroes are great because they inspire you, they motivate you. At the same time, though, they can set you back if you compare yourself to them too literally. It is hard to measure up to a Superhero...or is it?

I believe we are all superheroes…in different contexts, in different ways and in the eyes of different people. In the eyes of our children, we are heroes. Our jobs can garner; our generosity can make us guardian angels; and our teachers, our mentors, our coaches can be super in our eyes.

We all have our own set of what I call super powers…strengths that set each of us apart from others and, when combined, make us unique. And it is how you use your superpowers that determines how you live your life and how you impact the world.

It took me a while to discover my own super powers. And, to be honest, I tend to forget about them most of the time…until someone says something that brings it back to the forefront of my mind.

I used to think that what set me apart was my ability to juggle it all, to accomplish more in day than most people. I was **Professor Get it Done**. And sure, while completing a to-do list of the practical, the creative and the thoughtful brings value to my little world, it is neither what makes me unique nor what I should measure myself by.

Nope, I discovered two sets of "powers" that, when combined, have helped me make my mark in the world and, as it turns out, fuel me every day.

What has helped me most in my recent journey is my inner strength and my ability to meet a target once I lock my sights onto it. You remember these skills, right...the ones I carefully crafted in my youth? Well, I realized recently that they could come in handy as I placed a greater focus on my health. When you are battling an Eating Disorder, these abilities can be used for good (recovery, self-care, healthy eating) or "evil" (restriction, self-denial, unhealthy eating). It is all a matter of the goal you are setting.

When I first began treatment for my anxiety, depression and anorexia, most people around me were very positive and supportive. "You've got this," they said. They knew me for my determination and my ability to power-through anything. And, since I claimed I wanted to get well, no one doubted I could crack this. I was **Stiletto Dynamo** - a force to be reckoned with, especially given the 4-inch heels.

But, here is the thing, just as we each have our unique set of strengths, we also have our unique weaknesses. In my case, a strong disconnect between who I am and who I thought I was – coupled with a pesky anorexic voice in my brain – made things far more difficult than I had imagined. Turns out I was so disconnected from my real self that I had no idea how big my issues were, or how loud the anorexic voice was.

The day I started eating was the day I truly set my target to recovery while recognizing that there would be times when my target would shift to maintenance.

And, for the first time, I have the inner strength and support network to resist reverting back to my black and white thinking when I stumble. I am now able to stop myself from throwing in the towel and seeking refuge in full-fledged restriction when I am struggling. Why? Because the target remains recovery. And, while I can plateau, or take a step backward, reverting to the way I was before is no longer an option.

For a long time, this first set of skills is what I used to define myself, what made me proud. But, I eventually learned that I have a whole other tickle trunk of abilities – things that my friends and family appreciate most: energy, warmth, and an ability to engage and touch the spirit of those around me.

Connecting with people and having an impact on their lives is the thing that gives me the greatest satisfaction in my own life. I am not really sure how this all works, but somehow it seems to be the Peiky secret sauce.

Recently I was feeling frustrated about my accomplishments at work as a consultant. The deliverables were shifting, the expectations were being redefined after the fact and I felt I had nothing to show for my efforts. The achiever in me felt like I had failed to accomplish anything.

My boss took me aside and told me that when I first arrived, the client didn't want my team involved in the project and that most people didn't think I could pull it off. He then asked me to look around – the client loved us, my biggest adversaries at the onsetnow respected me and most people thought I had been a consultant for years.

He looked at me, shaking his head slightly: "and you don't think you accomplished anything?"

And, that, ladies and gentlemen, is how **Captain Peiky** does it.

Activity 12: Being Super

Define your inner superhero. Think about the things that people seem to appreciate about you, the positive feedback you receive, and try to identify a recurring theme. This is your super power. Have a bit of fun with this. Give yourself a name, draw out your costume, and keep it nearby for when you need a reminder of what you bring to the world.

Gladiatorin4inchheels.com

FINDING WONDER WOMAN

"About 2 months ago, I thought I had it all figured out. I knew better than the doctors; I wouldn't listen to my family and friends. I quit the Day Program I was in for Eating Disorders and I convinced myself that going back to work would fix everything. I would simply step back into my old life and all would be fine…like nothing ever happened. Good plan, right?

What I didn't count on was that my old life didn't exist anymore. Work had changed, people had changed, and without realizing it, I had changed. I thought if I could control my recovery, everything would fall into place.

I, Christina Peikert, Queen of options and plans, had a plan. And then, suddenly, I didn't. On the eve of my target return to work date, I was hit with the painful reality that my plan sucked. Big time.

Really? I was just gonna go back to work, where finding time to eat is a challenge, where stress is sky high and where naps (a daily occurrence for me at that time) are highly discouraged – even if you do it covertly under your desk.

Looking back, I have to laugh at how flawed my solution was but, at the time, it was devastating to see it all fall to pieces. I had worked so hard the previous 5 months scaling my own personal mountain and it turned out that all that work had only gotten me to the base. Scared and heartbroken, I had no idea how to start to climb again.

I had failed…and I had refused to see it coming. I felt lost and desperately wanted to give up. My friends rallied and took me to get help. I met a new psychiatrist, Fred, and for the first time, I truly felt understood and seen. He helped me start to reboot and find my fighting spirit.

And that is when I found Wonder Woman: a plastic doll I picked up in my friend's car and held in my lap as I left the hospital for the second time in 5 months after having suicidal thoughts (I am happy to say they are gone). Somehow she gave me the strength I need to take the first baby steps on my current path.

Gladiatorin4inchheels.com

I accepted to stay off work indefinitely. I started to work on self-love, on my desperate need for control and on living a life with no plan.

And right now, I am in a really good place.

I am happier than I have been for a while and I am going back to Day Treatment. Stay tuned for stories from there!

This new path began with Wonder Woman…who knows where it will lead.

But, if I had my pick, it would be to Ryan Reynolds as the Green Lantern!

RECOVERY CLUB

When you spend weeks with a group of women who are also undergoing treatment for an Eating Disorder, bonds between people inevitable form. During my two stints of treatment at the Douglas, I saw some people form strong friendships. Rumor even has it that a few love matches between patients have occurred during this type of treatment. You become a family, a support club to one another.

This is natural. Not only do you spend quite a bit of time together, opening yourself up in a way that few people ever do, but you also find a lot of commonality with the people around you. These women were intelligent, strong and kind.

And, most importantly, they understand.

They understand that it is not as simple as just eating. They understood the fear of reaching your weekly weight target but also being petrified to fall below it. They understand the discomfort brought on by a lunch of pizza AND dessert. They understand the inability to shut off the little hamster constantly running around in your brain.

When I left treatment at the Douglas, I was struggling. So, naturally, I felt a certain kinship with others that were struggling as well. They understood what is was like, at a time when it seemed like no one else ever could. But, the problem is that understanding is only one aspect of your support network. And, though it can seem like it is the most important part, it isn't. Don't get me wrong, it helps. My god does it help. I cannot tell you how many of my fellow patients had a positive impact on my life.

But, for someone to truly help you in the longer-term, they need to be available to help. Someone who is fighting for their own recovery may not have the energy, time, brain space to support you when you need it most. So it is important not to rely too much on your therapy group – in my humble, non-medical opinion – because what they bring in understanding may be outweighed by the demands of their own battles. In fact, you could find yourselves triggering each other's Eating Disorders and inadvertently causing harm.

When I left the Day hospital, I was deep in my relapse. I did not aspire to be part of the Recovery club. I was happy to be in the "treatment doesn't work" club. I turned to those around me who also had the same view because they understood what I was going through. I identified more with them because I knew that they were knee-deep in the battle just like me.

The problem for me was that I used their realities as examples that recovery was impossible. I allowed myself to use them to justify my relapse. After all, if these inspirational, strong women were struggling, what chance did I have? Turning to them for support was like wrapping myself in a warm blanket.... a safe, comfortable blanket of restriction. It felt good in the moment...but I knew it was not the solution.

I started to realize that I was not helping myself or those battling around me. So, I was forced to retreat for a while, keeping in touch with only a very small group of fellow ED Gladiators. But, there was a bit of an unspoken agreement that if I needed them, they would be there. And, if they needed me, I would drop everything without hesitation.

Eventually, I decided I did not want to be part of the Recovering club. I wanted to be part of the Recovered club. And, I knew that the only way to do that, was to change my behaviors. I realized that it is ok to be doing well, that the real friendships I made during my treatment were not bound by whether I was struggling or not. I would not be left behind just because I had moved forward in my journey to a healthy way of being...just as I would never walk away from my friends that won their own battles.

I had been thinking about this for a few weeks, when, one morning, I decided to take a step forward in my recovery. It was right around the time I went to the Crisis Center. Determined to eat more, I brought in a fruit to eat at the office in the morning – something I had not done in months.

After spending an hour debating about whether or not to eat the apple I brought, a constant dialogue in my head saying : "eat it, don't eat it, hide it in your purse, put it in the fridge so you are not tempted," I was texting a friend who was struggling. I understood perfectly what she was saying about her eating behaviors and thoughts. In fact, I was living a very similar pattern myself.

I felt empathy and compassion for her and I desperately wanted to help her. I wanted to suggest she speak with someone… someone who had recovered and who could help her find a new way but I was left empty-handed. It is hard to find people who have recovered. Sure, some have written books but a best-selling author is not a very accessible source of comfort and wisdom on a random Tuesday morning. Very few recovered patients come back to their treatment centers as advocates for recovery. As a result, I had no one to recommend for this friend.

And then it hit me, I could be a recovered person that speaks to others and helps them find their way. I could bring that mix of understanding and availability to support others. I could leverage my super power of engaging and impacting the people around me. IF…I…RECOVERED.

Hmmmm….this was a very compelling and inspiring thought. Maybe this was what I was supposed to do with the next phase of my life. It was not an easy mission to set for myself. But, I've never been one to shy away from a challenge (whether it be a dance off, a round of Jeopardy or a big project). Maybe I can heal I thought…and maybe, one day, I can share my story and help others heal as well.

Maybe… I thought to myself as I reached into my purse and bit into my apple.

Activity 13: Membership

This activity might be difficult to complete. And, it will likely offend some people. But, I like to end things with a bit of controversy.

Look at the people around you. Evaluate them honestly please because if you don't, this becomes a pointless exercise. Try to put each of these people into the following categories:

* Helpful to me right now
* Neutral
* Harmful to me right now
* Harmful to me always

You might feel uncomfortable with this because you may notice some names falling into a bucket you don't like. I get that – which is why I am building a bit of grey into this exercise. There are people who may be harmful to your recovery right now – perhaps because they are too deep in their own struggles or perhaps because they just can't support you at the moment.

These are people that you should consider creating space with. Maybe not forever…but at least for a little while. You can decide to see them less or to stop following their feeds on Facebook.

No need for a dramatic goodbye. In fact, in many cases, they never need to know you are taking a break from them. For example, there are some people I met during my treatment who are deep in their anorexia. Often, their Facebook Selfies are triggering for me because they awaken the voice in me that wants to be the "skinniest." So, I don't have them in my feed anymore but I still ask about them through my network to ensure they are continuing with their fight.

In some cases, you may need to explain to people why you have to distance yourself from them. For example, I think back to someone I became close to during my time in therapy. For a time, we communicated often and then, at one point, she told me she needed to go quiet for a bit. I respected that and she still pops up from time to time which I am thankful for.

The point here is that you have to identify the allies to your recovery and have them as lifelines while creating space with those who cannot help you right now. They may become allies at some point but, for now, leave them be while you work on yourself.

And, if you are telling yourself you need to keep in touch with them because they need your help, don't! You cannot help them right now. You need to help yourself. Then, one day, you may be able to be a great positive influence on their own recovery.

As for the people in the last category, I suggest you retreat, run, block and cut off. I found that the part of me that clung to my Eating Disorder likes to cling to things or people that can hurt me. As long as you leave space in your life for these harmful influences, you leave an opening for your Eating Disorder to exploit.

AWAKENING

I took a shower this morning! For most, this statement wouldn't cause anyone to bat an eyelash. In my house, this was news.

I have not taken a shower in months. Now, before you pinch your nose and scrunch your face up thinking « Ew », let me clarify that I take at least 2 baths daily and subscribe to only the highest standards of hygiene.

A few months ago, a dark fog set in around me. I struggled to get out of bed most days and standing up to take a shower took more effort than I had to give. I simply couldn't face the thought of doing it.

The last few months have been difficult and extremely hard to understand. I was eating more, fully settled at work and the weather was great. Why, then, was I feeling so low? The doctors said it was a phase – though no one could pinpoint the cause. Tests revealed I was physically healthy. So what gives?

I started to question my medication.

Antidepressants generate a lot of press…none of it is 100 percent conclusive. Studies range from saying they don't work to saying they play a critical role in the treatment of depression, to everything in between. And I suspect every study is accurate because the effectiveness of these medications varies as much as human beings do.

When I was first prescribed an antidepressant, I was at an all time low in terms of spirit and weight. I did not ask about the side effects and I didn't hesitate. I wanted something to help ensure I could keep on living.

As my mental health has improved – thanks to a lot of internal work, a huge support network and a loooooot of talking – I started to re-examine the role this medication played in my life.

The list of side effects it can trigger is extensive and the effectiveness can vary over time.

For me, the antidepressants had a bit of a numbing effect. They froze my sensations, my brain functions.

For a time, this was exactly what I needed as I focused heavily on developing coping mechanisms for my overactive brain and my erratic emotions.

Over time, though, this numbing effect started to have a harmful impact. I was exhausted, a novel concept for me, and I had zero interest in life. I did not look forward to things and I rarely experienced joy. I was sleepwalking through life but conscious of it. This plummeted me into a very dark time.

So, after much discussion with my partner in crime (Charles) and my psychiatrist, I recently started the process of weaning myself off my antidepressants.

I want to be clear: I firmly believe antidepressants serve a role and can bring much relief to many. I have no shame related to taking them and I believe they played a positive role in my journey back from the brink.

That said, I am a different person now, and I believe my body and brain are ready to bid them farewell.

This weaning process has to be done slowly, carefully and with the support of a mental health and medical professional as the medication alters your brain chemistry. Done too rapidly, and you can create the sensation of shocks to your brain. It is done in stages and, at each stage, you wait and watch for side effects – of which there can be many.

Week 1, no negative side effects but my energy started to return.

Week 2, my emotional and physical thaw really started to take effect. I felt happier, my brain was sharper from the moment I woke up. No more endless snoozing in the morning with no desire to get out of bed. At the same time though, my past impulsivity and negative self talk started to make an appearance. But, this time, I have coping mechanisms and a stronger, more informed support network to help.

I won't lie, seeing some of these emotions come back scares me. What will week 3 and 4 bring? Is this a sign of a trade off I will have to make in life: feeling energized and alive but emotionally unstable? Is there a happy medium to come? Will I be unable to recognize myself next week?

I don't know... Maybe I will mull it over, in the shower!

EPILOGUE

When I started this book, I had visions of where I would be when I finished. Call it delusions of grandeur but I really thought I would be fully recovered within the six months it took to tell my story. I had not anticipated the setbacks or the waves of depression I would face as my weight climbed. But, here I am…square in the recovery process, not yet able to wear my hard-earned recovery pin, yet smiling and proud.

Those who know me might look at where I am currently and conclude that I have merely come full circle from where I was 3 years ago: back to being a highly-functioning anorexic, someone who is underweight, living a busy life, juggling work, kids, family, friends and multiple responsibilities; someone who appears to have it all under control but who is managing a storm raging beneath the surface. To the people who believe this, I have one thing to say:

"Thank you!"

Thank you for recognizing that I am at this place – where I am not just functional...I am highly functional (this over achiever needs her shiny star please). Given the low points experienced in the last 2 years, I am so proud of where I am as I type this book. There were times where I was not sure I would be alive today. I am not saying this to be dramatic or to justify being satisfied with my progress. It is simply my truth. I went from a suboptimal place to extremely low depths and have spent almost 2 years fighting to make it back to this suboptimal place.

I would also say that, while, at first glance, it would appear I am at the same spot I used to be, this could not be further from the truth.

Sure, there are similarities between both stages but I know beyond a shadow of a doubt that I have surpassed where I was a few years ago. I know this is not Square One because:

* I have learned... I have picked up key nuggets of knowledge along my journey. I am now aware of my triggers and know when I am falling into old patterns. I may not always be able to avoid these, but being able to identify them helps me course correct or, in some cases, accept help from others in my network who have a heightened awareness about my illness.

* I am stronger… I have developed new coping mechanisms for my anxiety. I color or meditate when I feel my nerves start to jangle. I go to the bathroom if I need a quick break from a meeting that I find too frustrating. I tolerate.

* I operate at reduced speed… I am now able to go for a stroll (rather than the fast Peiky-pace I used to walk at), I can sit still for a few minutes at a time; and I can leave the laundry for tomorrow.

* I am calmer…when my obsessive thoughts start to run through my mind, I can actually acknowledge what they are, remind myself that they are not useful and focus on something else. Ok, often, the only thing that enables me to stop the thoughts is to sing – apologies to people I come across on the street, in the park, and in my car. Still, it is a step in the right direction.

* I am off anti-depressants…not because they did not work or are bad for you. On the contrary, they served a very important purpose early on in my recovery and play a critical role in the lives of many people. Simply, right now, I no longer need them as part of my daily life.

* I can sleep... I come home after a tough day at work, where emotions ran high, and go to bed easily rather than being up half the night, analyzing, overthinking and developing a plan to fix things that really don't need fixing.

* I taste...I now try foods from my forbidden list. Not always, but sometimes, in the middle of the day, with people around. God bless my colleague and her Baklava.

* I can weigh myself, shrug and say "Fuck it" and go about my day without it being ruined by the number I saw.

* I enjoy where I am...I have balance now. I work for a company that respects my boundaries and, when I contemplate the future, I no longer seek out the VP title I once did.

* I am authentic...I can admit my needs and readjust my expectations. There is no greater proof of this than the fact that I am putting this book out there even though I fell short of my original objective of being recovered.

Is there a lot of work left to be done? Absolutely! Am I ready to earn my "Recovered" badge? I am not sure. But, if I look hard enough, I can see that next level. I can close my eyes and describe it and, on my best days, aspire to live it.

There are lots of questions left to be answered and I don't know exactly what comes next. The Old Me would find this lack of certainty troubling; Current Me is ok with this.

Why?

Quite simply because I know that no matter how it plays out, when I am ready to move to the Recovered zone, 2 things are certain.

     1- I will not be going there alone; and

     2- I am going to take a flying leap to get there.

THE ENCORE

THEN

I started restricting again.
I pretended everything was fine.
I lost weight.
I smiled.

I felt weak.
I stopped dancing.
I started crawling.
But I still smiled.

I stopped eating.
I withdrew.
I lied.
I stopped smiling.

I embraced the darkness.
I broke down.
I wound up at the ER.
I spent days living in a Crisis Center.

NOW

The past 4 weeks have been life-changing.

It has been ONE MONTH since my last restriction.

The story is being written. One minute, one moment, one mouthful at a time.

Stay tuned.

(Note: blog written a month after I started eating and when I started this book)

REFERENCES

The Eating Disorders Program (EDP) at the Douglas Mental Health University Institute offers specialized clinical services for people 18 years and older who suffer from anorexia nervosa or bulimia nervosa. Quebec's largest and best-developed program for people with EDs, the EDP offers informed treatments for people with severe EDs. (http://www.Douglas.QC.ca/section/eating-disorders-146)

The Douglas Institute is part of the Centre intégré universitaire de santé et de services sociaux (CIUSSS) de l'Ouest-de-l'Île-de-Montréal. (http://www.Douglas.QC.ca/section/about-us-345)

The West Island Crisis Center is a non-profit, community-based organization that provides free and specialized crisis intervention services 24 hours a day, 7 days a week (www.centredecriseoi.com)

BIBLIOGRAPHY

The following books were important reading as part of my recovery process.

Costin, Carolyn & Schubert Grabb, Gwen. 8 *Keys to Recovery from an Eating Disorder: Effective Strategies from Therapeutic Practice and Personal Experience.* W.W. Norton & Company, 2011. Print.

Doyle, Glennon. *Love Warrior.* Flatiron Books, 2016. Print

Doyle Melton, Glennon. *Carry on, Warrior: The Power of Embracing Your Messy, Beautiful Life.* Simon and Schuster, 2013. Print

Hamilton, David R. *I Heart Me: The Science of Self-Love.* Hay House, Inc., 2015. Print

Johnson, Amy. *The Little Book of Big Change.* New Harbinger Publications, 2016. Print.

Lancer, Darlene. *Codependency for Dummies.* Wiley, 2012. Print

Manson, Mark. *The Subtle Art of Not Giving a Fuck: A Counterintuitive Approach to Living a Good Life.* Harper, 2016. Print

Parkin, John. *F*ck it. Do what you love.* Hay House UK Limited, 2016. Print

Ravikant, Kamal. *Love Yourself Like your Life Depends on It.* CreateSpace Independent Publishing Platform, 2012. Print & eBook.

Rhimes, Shonda. *Year of Yes: How to Dance It Out, Stand in the Sun and Be Your Own Person.* Simon and Schuster, 2016. Print

Schaefer, Jenni. *Life Without Ed.* McGraw Hill Professional, 2003. Print

Schaefer, Jenni. *Goodbye Ed, Hello Me.* McGraw Hill Professional, 2009. Print

ABOUT THE AUTHOR

The daughter of a chef and a picky eater from birth, Christina Peikert first began her battle with anorexia at the age of 23; and spent 17 years living with an Eating Disorder before seeking treatment. For almost 2 decades, she was a high-functioning anorexic with an established career in Marketing and Communications and an uncanny ability to pretend everything was ok.

She has been a Marketing and Communications Director, a Consultant, a Coach, a Leader, a Blogger, a Mother and now a Writer.

She lives in Vaudreuil-Dorion, Quebec with her husband and two daughters.

The Day I Started Eating is her debut novel. More information and her blog can be found at gladiatorin4inchheels.com